Better Together

Jonathan Sposato

Better Together

8 Ways Working with Women Leads to Extraordinary Products and Profits

WILEY

Published by John Wiley & Sons, Inc., Hoboken, New Jersey
Published simultaneously in Canada

For general information about our other products and services, please contact our Customer Care
Department within the United States at (800) 762-2974, outside the United States at (317) 572-3993
or fax (317) 572-4002.

Wiley publishes in a variety of print and electronic formats and by print-on-demand. Some material
included with standard print versions of this book may not be included in e-books or in
print-on-demand. If this book refers to media such as a CD or DVD that is not included in the
version you purchased, you may download this material at http://booksupport.wiley.com. For more
information about Wiley products, visit www.wiley.com.

Library of Congress Cataloging-in-Publication Data is Available:

ISBN 9781119452188 (Hardcover)
ISBN 9781119452133 (ePDF)
ISBN 9781119452089 (ePub)

Cover Design: Wiley
Cover Image: © Luciano Lozano /Getty Images

Printed in the United States of America.

10 9 8 7 6 5 4 3 2 1

Contents

Foreword

Jonathan SPO-SA-TO. Before you even meet him you are thinking it's totally going to be a different guy. Italian last name, Asian face. What is *that* story?

It's like picking up this book and saying "Wait a minute. Why is a middle-aged dude writing a book (which will inevitably make him a target for haters) passionately making the case for gender equity in the workplace? What gives him the right? What makes him special?"

Well, I would argue, Sposato has the right. He has earned it. Jonathan's experiences, starting with the circumstances of his birth, make him very uniquely qualified to address any issues surrounding bias and inequity. He has lived the struggle, and he walks the walk. I often jokingly refer to him as "Asian Obama."

It's not just that Jonathan is an uber-successful businessman, founder, investor, husband, and dad who supports women 150 percent. He's really taking on gender workplace inequity as an individual who cares deeply about *inclusivity*. "Inclusivity" is part of Jonathan's DNA.

Jonathan's whole existence has been about beating the odds. He is someone who has been rejected and accepted throughout his life: separated from his biological father but accepted, loved, and raised by a single mother and later an adopted father. From age 3, Jonathan survived six years without his single mom because she couldn't afford to raise him. When he finally rejoined her in the 1970s, he was brought into and raised in a mixed-race household and had to learn to fit in.

He had to push his way in through his positivity, charm, openness, inclusivity, and willingness to listen to people and understand where they are coming from and build bridges. It's what made him originally a great entrepreneur.

Jonathan's leadership style focuses on what's best for all involved, what's always a win for all parties. It's been a huge part of his success building great software that people love and great businesses that are successful in their communities because he works hard to understand the community and give them what they care about.

Without Jonathan, our company may not have existed. At first, he couldn't believe my story of being a female CEO consistently rejected for funding. He heard me out and he didn't write it off. He remembered our time together at Microsoft, and, ultimately, he invested in me and our company because he did believe in us. He couldn't let it rest. He couldn't just sit by and accept that a pattern bias of not funding qualified female founders was the norm.

Because Jonathan has dealt firsthand with issues of inclusivity in his own life, any kind of social injustice or inequity is an issue that he will not tolerate in his businesses, on his teams, and in his environments. What he stands for as an individual is inclusivity. Let the best rise to the top no matter who they are. I am perfectly comfortable with having him speak out on behalf of *all* of us who suffer bias. Although we are primarily talking about women right now, we are in an increasingly diverse culture, and if our products and services and environments are going to reflect who we are, they must be built by all of us.

Jonathan has as much right to tell this story as any one of us, and I'm honored to be included in Jonathan's book.

Lisa Maki
CEO of PokitDok

With Grace Kahng

This book would not have happened without Grace Kahng, who catalyzed the notion that there was a book here. She strategized, congealed, debated, and refined so much of what is BEST about this book. She conducted countless interviews with many people whom I wouldn't have thought to ask, imbued this project with energy, recalibrated my thinking on numerous themes, and bravely authored chapter 7 when i asked her to, as well as helping fix a couple of mine.

Her editorial instincts are nothing short of masterful, refining and reshaping cloddish ideas into those worthy of publication. She is the very model of the kind of effective blended leadership that I speak of, and I honestly don't know how she does what she does so dang well, all the time. She is also, in strength, values, and work ethic, the very embodiment of the kind of "baller women" that this book is about. Anyone would be lucky to have Grace Kahng on her team.

About the Author

A successful serial entrepreneur and investor in many startups, Jonathan Sposato is chairman and cofounder of GeekWire.com, one of the tech sector's top news sites, and chairman and cofounder of PicMonkey, the world's most fun and popular photo editor.

He also has the distinct honor of being the first person to sell two companies to Google.

In 2016, Jonathan made headlines when he announced he would be the first technology investor to invest *only* in female-founded companies moving forward. This put Jonathan in the national spotlight, and he became an honoree of various women-led organizations such as American Women in Science, Vital Voices, and the University of Washington ("Man of Integrity" award). He has invested in many startups founded by women, such as Pokitdok, Glamhive, GiftStarter, Runway2Street, Poppy, Scout, Vivifi, and others. Jonathan is also a key investor and "Distinguished Entrepreneur in Residence" at the groundbreaking women's co-working space The Riveter.

Sposato recently handed over the CEO responsibilities of PicMonkey to a successor in order to dedicate himself to the mission of developing, identifying, and promoting more female representation and leadership in business.

Jonathan is also the founder of WeCount.org, the first nonprofit to apply smartphone technologies to help people who are homeless receive items critical to their survival on the streets. Jonathan was awarded the "Innovation and Equity Award" from Seattle's mayor in 2016.

Prior to all this, Jonathan cofounded Picnik.com and created the first profitable online photo subscription service, reaching over 60 million visitors a month. Prior to Picnik, Jonathan founded Phatbits, which went on to become Google Gadgets.

In the early 1990s, Jonathan was a senior manager in Microsoft's consumer division, personally delivering the next level of thought on key Microsoft properties to Chairman Bill Gates and the company's leadership, as well as having been a key player on the first Xbox, the Xbox games business, and various consumer applications that impact millions of users.

Jonathan is a graduate of Whitman College, where he is on the board of trustees.

Introduction

Sister, Where Art Thou?

Women. Over half of the earth's population, and creators of life for the whole of it. They are our mothers, wives, daughters, and colleagues. Women account for 85 percent of all spending, arguably the expression of true power. And yet, if you survey the landscape of founders who've created the most successful tech companies of recent years—all males. Zuckerberg, Dorsey, Cheskey, Kalanick, Spiegel: captains of Facebook, Twitter, Airbnb, Uber, Snapchat. Revolutionary founders who have created massively valuable companies that affect billions. It clearly appears to be the sport of men.

Is it just a coincidence that there are so few women at the top? Only 24 female CEOs lead America's Fortune 500. And in tech, female-founded companies are only 3 percent of all startups funded by venture capitalists. Are we to believe that women simply don't create great things? Or should we finally acknowledge that we operate in an unfair system where the path for women in business, leadership, and entrepreneurship is much, much harder. As an angel investor in startup companies I routinely hear amazing pitches from female entrepreneurs. In 2015, I pledged to only invest in tech startups with at least one female cofounder. Yet, in 2017, women are still not getting funded or promoted at the same rate as men, and the refrain from every female entrepreneur is consistent: *women are pushing a larger rock up a steeper hill.*

Women's lack of power and broader success in technology is simply a microcosm of what's happening in the larger world. Over the years, I've heard a myriad of excuses. It's a pipeline problem. Women aren't good at tech. They just don't think that way. They're too cautious. They aren't risk takers. Of course, that's a bunch of hogwash. Women aren't given equal leadership opportunities. Often, female leaders aren't given the same support their male peers receive to ensure success. But it doesn't have to be that way. We can and must do better.

And the whole "pipeline problem" is an all-too-convenient excuse. First, more than half of all college graduates today are women. In the fields of law and medicine, women outnumber men and yet represent just a fraction of the partners and chair positions compared to men. Within STEM degrees in particular, the percentage of female graduates has been steadily approaching 50 percent over the past two decades. Furthermore, the Small Business Administration has estimated that 7.8 million U.S. businesses have been started and are owned by women, representing a stunning 44 percent increase since the 1990s and at twice the growth rate of male-owned businesses. This is a heartening statistic that testifies to women's strength, vision, and leadership abilities.*

I strongly assert that if your company or your team has very few women in the workforce, and few women in positions of leadership, then you are part of the problem I am inviting you to solve.

And what *is* that problem exactly? The first problem lies in the fact that men in positions of power (venture, boardrooms, C-suites, management) may not be acknowledging that a problem actually exists. Some believe we live in a meritocracy. "See? There are no women leaders at my company

---

*There are some in engineering like my good friend and Evertoon CEO Niniane Wang who cite that it is still highly difficult to find a greater gender balance (say, 50-50) in software development. Even when Google redirected one-third of all recruiters to focus solely on sourcing female engineers, that only brought up the percentage from 13 percent to 19 percent. And while when I speak generally about all functional areas when I say that there is no longer a pipeline issue, I grant that in engineering there may still be a larger lag between the much higher percentages of women graduating with computer science degrees today and the actual percentages of women writing code in the industry. I do believe, as others do, that this gap is continuing to narrow, and that it is the existence of this gap that indicates that the issue is still more about friction for women in the pipeline versus lack of available talent.

because so few have earned it!" And many acknowledge there is a problem, but just don't know what to do.

I believe that we must all take responsibility for our role in this situation. All of us. That includes the men in power who don't recognize the problem or take concrete actions to solve it. It includes a *few* women who likewise refuse to see how they might harbor their own unconscious biases against other women. It includes everyone at every level, in the tech industry and in all industries, who still sees women's lack of power and opportunity as a problem with their innate abilities rather than the result of conscious/unconscious bias and cultural and institutional barriers.

The goal of this book is to provide managers, CEOs, board members, and business owners a blueprint to attract, recruit, hire, and build a sustainable gender-balanced workforce at all levels. It's not only the right thing to do, it's the smart thing to do.

1. You will learn how to create a gender-balanced team, workforce, or company.
2. You will become fully informed on all issues of gender equity, gaining a holistic view based on recent gender communication research, latest recruitment practices, history of gender legislation to date and how it impacts industry, as well as firsthand insights drawn from individuals' making current headlines on gender issues.
3. You will become a better leader, helming a gender-balanced workforce that creates better products, increasing profitability, improving retention, and reducing costs. Learning how to create a gender-balanced workforce by reading this book is simply great for the bottom line.
4. With women driving about 85 percent of all purchasing decisions in the United States, it's critical for companies to give women a greater seat at the table when it comes to every aspect of their operations. And, as we'll discuss, your business will improve markedly with more women on staff and in power.

What Do I Know about Women?

Of course, the next obvious question is, "Why me?" Why is a 50-year-old *male* entrepreneur and CEO penning a book about women? When I became the first person to sell two tech companies to Google (I was more lucky than good), I saw how my own gender-balanced teams of men and women outperformed other companies. One of those companies, Picnik.com, was a photo-editing service that captured more than 60 million unique users a month at its peak. I assert Picnik's success was the direct result of our near 50-50 female-male team composition. The gender balance contributed to the "special sauce" and collaborative environment that birthed a beautifully executed product that resonated at scale. Bottom line: in my experience, when women and men work together as equals the products and services they create are simply much better.

> Today the tech industry does not look like America, and that has a significant influence on the types of products and services that get created. When the lived experience of underrepresented communities is omitted from the product development cycle, the usefulness of the technology becomes biased towards one group. —The Kapor Capital Founders' Commitment

GeekWire.com, a technology news site that I financed and cofounded with two much more brilliant partners in 2009, grew to millions in page views a month and more than 10 tentpole events annually in just its third year (we're now in our seventh), exactly because great care was taken to write technology stories that are relevant to everyone (not just male tech employees) and to make each of our events highly female friendly. Our intent was to "do tech differently." It is no surprise that our events are routinely remarked upon as the most gender inclusive in tech with industry high percentages of female speakers and attendees.

When women are present, **_great things happen_**. Recent research conducted by Credit Suisse indicates that shares of companies in which women make up more than 33 percent of senior management roles had a higher average annualized return (25.6 percent vs. 22 percent) than companies with only 25 percent female managers. The Peterson Institute of International Economics reports in a 2016 study that having at least 30 percent of women in leadership positions, or the C-suite, adds another 6 percent to net profit margin. Even more astounding, data from Quontopian, a trading platform based on crowdsourced algorithms, shows that the 80 female CEOs they followed during a 12-year study (2002–2014) produced equity returns 226 percent better than the S&P 500. All in all, the research shows that teams and management exhibiting greater gender balance outperform more homogeneous ones.

It's Personal

Another reason I'm writing this book is much more personal. As a child born out of wedlock in the 1960s, I witnessed the struggles of my immigrant single mother trying to juggle raising a child, hold a full-time job, and earn the respect of her male colleagues. Ultimately, she felt she was failing me. When I was 3 years old, one of my few early memories is watching my mother's face disappear from the backseat of a NYC Yellow Cab. She sent me to Hong Kong to live with my maternal grandparents and strangers that I had never met.

"It was the most difficult decision of my life and I have to live with that pain for every day of my life," my mother recently shared. I try not to discuss the past with her in part because what lives and breathes in the unspoken absence of time between us still holds a great deal of power and sorrow.

Born in Hong Kong in 1938 as the oldest of five children, my mother Helena left home at the age of 17 for London seeking to create a better future for herself. This was an extremely bold life choice for a teenage girl at that time. She made that decision because she knew that a Chinese girl in the twentieth century exists to first serve her parents and later, a husband. She experienced and understood the great disadvantage that many Asian women experience as a result of gender. She says that despite being the oldest child, her youngest brother enjoyed a higher status than she did. He was sent to a better school, held in higher regard by their parents, and was the designated heir to the family textiles business. For my mother, going West was a way to eschew the old world for a more progressive and fuller life. An education in London or New York represented not only a ticket out of Hong Kong but an escape from a sexist system where girls and women could never get ahead.

My mother says even though she excelled at her work as a nurse, it wasn't a career she necessarily enjoyed because of the lack of respect nurses were afforded by the male doctors and medical staff. It was under these circumstances that she found herself pregnant by a young resident. Instead of asking family friends and relatives in New York City for help, Helena quietly disappeared to London to give birth. When she returned to New York City she did her best to cope with working full time and raising a son. But the burden of being a single working parent with no family support in a foreign country proved too much. My mother says that as my grandmother whisked me away in that cab, my screams and tears nearly broke her.

It would be six long years before my mother would hold my face again.

With great love and admiration for my grandparents who provided me with a loving home and a rigorous parochial education at Rosary Hill Academy in Hong Kong, I often joke that I was an American kid from Brooklyn going to a British school full of Chinese kids being taught how to sing in broken-English by Spanish nuns. I think I was the embodiment of an "outsider." It didn't help my keen awareness that I was very different or "less than," that my classmates would question why my "parents" were so old or constantly ask where my parents were. These were not questions I could answer because I wondered the same thing.

By the time I returned to America, my mother had established her nursing career, married a good man with a master's degree in hospital administration from Princeton, and bought a house. She says that she didn't feel that she could send for me until she had achieved her vision of the American dream of creating a stable home. These early experiences made me pay attention to women's struggles.

★ ★ ★

In addition to my mother's own trials, I also saw the challenges endured by my Aunt Bette, a female entrepreneur in Silicon Valley in the early 1980s when there were few entrepreneurs of any gender. Back then, entrepreneurs were known as oddballs who opted out of the norm of the corporate world.

There was no playbook for her, except for one to be a dutiful wife and daughter. She had no role model for a female CEO. She had to break one mold and create a whole new one. She partnered with her husband, my industrious uncle Patrick, to start a computer hardware assembly and testing company. The company eventually grew to supply many of Silicon Valley's brand-name manufacturers as well as multinational operations overseas. Her charisma with clients, approachable demeanor with employees, and focused ambition were the key reasons their business thrived when others failed.

Of course, my incomparable Uncle Patrick also played a role in the company's success. After quitting his job at IBM, he worked tirelessly for a year as a real estate agent in order to scrape together the $100,000 they would need for seed capital. As a young teen working summers at their plant, I became convinced that the combination of very uniquely male and female skill sets made them a winning team. They were "better together."

Last, I'm also writing this book because I had to overcome odds as an "outsider," too. Growing up Asian in an all-white, working-class community of Edmonds, Washington, in the 1970s brought stigma and shame in an America that had just endured three brutal wars against the "yellow man." I remember being kicked off of my bicycle and being spat on by a stranger who shouted: "My brother died in 'Nam!" Being called every racial slur except for the correct one was commonplace during my awkward tween years, and after a while I stopped correcting them.

No one at my school *looked* like me. TV and comic books offered no solace either. The only Asians in the media were Don Ho, Connie Chung, and later Mr. Miyagi from *The Karate Kid*. And while being an Asian *girl* might have granted one greater social mobility, to be an Asian boy meant an entire childhood of playing the role of the "Indian," the "Viet Cong," or "the bad guy" on the playground. I realized I would never be Captain America. And in all this, I began to understand the system of currency at work—a system of currency that I would later put to work in my favor.

As I grew older, I recognized that I might be living in a slightly rigged system, where certain people got ahead much more easily, while others didn't have as good a chance. I watched as my friends' fathers did business with their golfing friends or their families would take vacations together. Yet my interracial parents were never invited.

I understood that getting into a good school meant scoring high on the SATs, with a letter of recommendation from a pillar of the community. But most immigrant children didn't know words of the privileged like "vestibule" or "foyer," and even lesser connection with community influencers. It was as if the system helped the privileged maintain privilege. To this day, the United States is the only country in the world where it's easier to get into a top-10 institution if one of your parents happened to go there. A rigged system indeed.

In adulthood, I again felt like an outsider because I didn't fit the standard mold—the type A male boss. I was often told early in my career I was "too nice," "too people oriented," "over focused on consensus," and needed to be more of an "ass kicker." And, yet, I would eventually attain more success than I deserved, through an inspiring leadership style that incorporated both results-driven and nurturing qualities.

I assumed as time passed and people evolved that the world would just get better and better for women. But with headline after headline detailing the ridiculous behavior of individual men toward female colleagues or woeful statistics on the gender pay gap or lack of female executives, it's tough not to be seriously discouraged about the lack of progress. As an angel investor in many tech startups, female entrepreneurs have shared disheartening and sexist stories about their struggles to raise the same amount of money as their male counterparts but always falling short or never getting started at all. This is not fair, not today.

I know that some may see me as unfairly characterizing men as the bad guys, impugning all white men or all men with certain titles or all women who don't consider themselves feminists. *That's not my intention. I believe we're all inheritors of a broken system that we did not ourselves create.* But until we step out of its context and take stock of how a flawed system is sustained by our inaction, we're all guilty parties to its continuance—myself included. It's like being inside the matrix, you don't know how bad it is until someone unplugs you. But first YOU have to take the red pill.

As someone who understands firsthand how cultural norms and unjust stereotypes can hold people back, I feel strongly about helping to fix the problem. If we are to finally carry the ball over the goal line regarding gender equality, we need to change our culture, processes, and even our national priorities. In the same way that attitudes about climate change, same-sex marriage, and civil rights have all made a radical about-face, companies and political leaders need to **think differently** and **adopt an active strategy** to take much bigger steps toward the goal of gender equity. This can only happen when boardrooms, CEOs, investors, and recruiters acknowledge and address the problem. While some have started to at the margins, most of corporate America is still vastly behind. I write this as a call to action for all of us, men and women, to join together in the fight for gender equity. We can be better together.

Jonathan and his mother, Helena, in 1968.

Source: Author's own.

I Know We Can Do Better

The tech sector I come from is merely a contemporary reflection of decades-old problems with gender equality and women's rights across all business segments. I write this book because I *know* we can all do better. I write this book because I know *how* we can do better. And I write this book because it is time for the hard truths to be acknowledged, for the hard work to begin. And that's what's most beautiful about America I think. We have an unstoppable talent as Americans to retool, reinvent, reboot, and adapt. Let's be "better together."

Maria Hess
Head of Business Development, Growth and Marketing, PicMonkey

Straight Talk: "Ask yourself why you use the phrase "working mother" but never use that phrase to describe "working father." Why do we need to call out working mothers differently? Or even acknowledge they're moms when we rarely do that for men? Yes, it could be said with good intentions, but I believe it's heard by others as the woman having diminished capacity and priority. I feel like what happens in the workplace today is more subtle or said in code, given a somewhat heightened awareness and training about gender equality."

1

Men Must Change

1992. Redmond, Washington. Consumer Division. Building 17.

I remember walking the halls of Building 17 in the middle of the night, just days before the deadline for shipping a product, the unmistakable smell of stale pizza in the air, combined with the whiff of half-a-dozen unwashed engineers pulling their third all-nighter.

The early 1990s were heady days for us young punks working in tech. The average age of a Microsoft employee at the time was about 29, but it felt like 19. And the population was overwhelmingly male and almost all white. In between muddy afternoon soccer matches in front of Building 8 and impromptu runs to the local Godfather's restaurant to play grease-buttoned Asteroids, we worked our butts off creating the most innovative technology solutions to everyday problems.

Inventing new product categories was my personal specialty. After abruptly chickening out of law school, I started a games company, which grew to 42 employees at the beginning of the "software renaissance." We made some of the very first games on the Nintendo, Sega, and NEC consoles, each project an exploration in new gaming experiences. When I came to Microsoft to get a "real job," my projects were an interactive TV

1

show for kids, a web-based episodic comic book in which the pages spoke to you, and eventually the first game console that could push 124,000 polygons per second. We were changing the world one ship cycle at a time, years before Google, Amazon, or Facebook.

One colleague, who was an engineering rock star would routinely spar with CEO "billg" during meetings—and *win*. "No Bill, I think YOU are confused. And here's why...." We learned that loud and assertive was good. Might was right, and bravado ruled the roost. My friend, whose father was a retired engineer at Boeing, never missed an opportunity to remind his dad that our upstart software company that made the future out of thin air and brainpower boasted a higher market cap than the leading aerospace company of seven decades and billions in hard assets. Our stock option grants made us multimillionaires in our twenties, and the ideas we

Douglas Coupland's poignant capture of Microsoft's early culture.

pitched got funded and became divisions. We sincerely believed ourselves to be a *true* meritocracy, and the seeds of "brogrammer" culture were sown.

There were very few female colleagues working on products with us, so when we dated, we looked aspirationally to the "HR babes" in Building 24. They were refined, pretty, and smart while we languished in a man-child state. We treated them with a sort of geeky reverence. When one walked into the room, the energy would change palpably. We intuitively stopped being complete dorks and occasionally old-fashioned Edwardian-like romances budded. To this day, I smile when I see some of these still-married couples. And the few amazing women who were in management, leading product, or on technical teams, most of them knew better than to waste their time on us. They dated up in the stratosphere and deservedly so.

Welcome to Man Island

Then starting in the mid-1990s, we began to notice that the women at all levels in product groups started to leave, but we couldn't figure out why. Looking back, it's obvious: the culture was becoming unfriendly. For example, during an exhaustive candidate search for an open position, I recall one meeting with a male group manager who brashly stated his preference for the type of program manager leader we needed to hire: "I want to hear his balls clacking when he walks down the hall!"

Rather than being a conventional computer nerd, I was a scholar athlete who varsity lettered and was voted student body president. I generally traversed all social strata—friends with jocks, stoners, and computer lab geeks alike. At Microsoft, my photo was used in their recruiting brochure for several years, while I was routinely tapped to do public presentations on stage with CEO Bill Gates as a sort of amicable young company spokesperson. I enjoyed demoing new product offerings to developers, financial analysts, and movie studio execs with humor and lightheartedness not often associated with Microsoft's staid corporate persona. I remember thinking, "We're starting to become cool, coming out of geekdom." But, at the same time, in the then fast-growing games group, I saw some colleagues' offices down the hall be adorned with posters of big-busted female characters from video games. A few of these guys routinely compared notes on whose booth at E3 had the hottest models. At the lowest point, one shocking team meeting in the division cafeteria featured scantily clad "nurses" passing out Jello shots as a sort of morale booster. Facepalm.

Amid this budding "bro culture," some product divisions started to fall below a critical mass threshold of 13 to 15 percent women, entering a gender-biased death spiral the team would never recover from. The percentage of consumer products commissioned by the company targeted to women grew less and less. Gone were the Lifestyle Products Division, the Kids & Games Product Unit, and things like Encarta were defunded. There was no slide in anyone's PowerPoint deck that said, "Let's be a bunch of guys making products for guys." Yet that's what happened in certain divisions of the company. They were great teams with great leaders, but something was wrong. As one female colleague after another left, I wondered: Which came first, the chicken or the egg? Were women leaving because there were so few women wanting to join? Or were women afraid to join the division because they could see women were leaving?

The Sad Truth of the Here and Now

It's now 2017 and things don't seem better; they seem worse. Workplace culture at some of the high-valued new economy companies such as Uber, Snap, or Binary Capital has been highly unfriendly to women, bolstered by a new crop of male leaders who seem to have taken us back in time. And while most men in positions of leadership do not create horrible cultures, it is the overall tolerance for the bad outliers that allows institutionalized sexism to affect us all, even if we are certain we can't be sexist.

To better understand the very special way that sexism occurs in tech from a successful woman's perspective, Linda Kozlowski offers a position rooted in social dynamics between women and men during their formative young adult years. Kozlowski is a veteran tech executive who worked at Alibaba and now serves as chief operating officer of Etsy. She explains what she calls the "dork" factor in Silicon Valley, from the perspective of being a self-admitted female dork.

Tech overall is a very new industry. If you were in the 80s and writing a book about lawyers or Wall Street, the debauchery and the ridiculousness that you would see was just as insane. Ultimately it's a male-dominated workforce and tech is mainly made up of two main groups of people to start: (1) computer scientists or someone studying engineering or some kind of science that tends to be more male, and (2) the MBA set, which is changing but historically has definitely been more male.

It starts with this idea that you definitely hire people who look like you. When everyone in the company is younger to start, that's only exacerbated. Now let's add in another dynamic. You are incredibly awkward. You probably weren't that popular in high school or anything else. You were a dork. And, by the way, I'm dorky, so this is not an insult.

In college you are *encouraged* to hit on that girl. That's what college is about. You are going to parties. You see a cute girl in class and hitting on this girl is perfectly sanctioned and acceptable. You aren't working with that person. You are in class with them. You are encouraged to the *n*th degree to go and hit on this girl (assuming that you are straight). She's probably a little dorky herself. And suddenly you're starting to meet more and more people who are like you and the environment is like: "You should meet a girl like yourself. You should go to parties. You should hang out and have fun." That's the environment. There are no professional boundaries in the school environment.

So you get spit out of college as a computer science major, and you go straight into a big successful tech company where they are paying you a ton of money. All of a sudden you have power. You are in Silicon Valley where engineers are king. So you've gone from dork four years ago to Homecoming King, getting paid a ton of money. You're sitting next to those same women you were in class with, and what do you do? So, why are we shocked that this is happening?

Why are we shocked? This is something that the gender dynamic changes over time. It requires parents teaching different skills. This goes back to: are you given a doll or are you given a truck? There is so much of this that is formed from a very early age.

Kozlowski also attributes the amount of sexual harassment in tech to the fact that startups are antiestablishment. And often tech employees aren't formally mandated to attend diversity and inclusion workshops, safe-space training sensitivity, or workplace habit training that most Fortune 500 or established companies require. In fact, she says the culture of startups with their emphasis on youth tend to bristle at the notion of doing anything that is considered traditional.

Example A of male tone-deaf behavior is an email sent from former Uber CEO Travis Kalanick to his entire company in the early heady days after Uber's very successful launch. Today the company is valued at $60–$70 billion and has revolutionized personal transportation. Behind closed doors, Uber had created a dysfunctional culture unfriendly to women and men alike. Even 20 years ago, talk of drunkenness and sex with coworkers would have seemed unconscionable. We have taken a huge step backward indeed. (Bold highlights below are my emphasis.)

| ---------- Forwarded message ---------- |
| From: Travis Kalanick |
| Date: Friday, October 25, 2013 |
| Subject: 九 Info: URGENT, URGENT - READ THIS NOW OR ELSE!!!!! |
| To: Uber Team |
| Hey guys, I wanted to get some important information out there. I've put together a Q&A that we can use when other folks ask what we're doing here, and have some DOs and DON'Ts for our time here in Miami. |
| You better read this or I'll kick your ass. |
| _____ |
| I have gotten a list of concerns from the legal department. I have translated these concerns into a clear set of common sense guidelines. I've also added a few items of my own. |
| DON'Ts: |
| 1) No lives should begin or end at 九 |
| 2) We do not have a budget to bail anyone out of jail. Don't be that guy. #CLM |
| **3) Do not throw large kegs off of tall buildings. Please talk to Ryan McKillen and Amos Barreto for specific insights on this topic.** |

4) Do not have sex with another employee UNLESS a) you have asked that person for that privilege and they have responded with an emphatic "YES! I will have sex with you" AND b) the two (or more) of you do not work in the same chain of command. Yes, that means that Travis will be celibate on this trip. #CEOLife #FML

5) Drugs and narcotics will not be tolerated unless you have the appropriate medicinal licensing.

6) There will be a $200 puke charge for any public displays on the Shore Club premises. Shore Club will be required to send pictures as proof.

7) DO NOT TALK TO PRESS. Send all press inquiries to Andrew - anoyes@uber.com Additionally, stay vigilant about making sure people don't infiltrate our event. If and when you find yourself talking to a non–Uber (look for the wristband), keep confidential stuff confidential . . . no rev figures, driver figures, trip figures . . . don't talk about internal process, and don't talk about initiatives that have not already launched.

———————

DOs:

1) Have a great fucking time. This is a celebration! We've all earned it.

2) Share good music. Digital DJs are encouraged to share their beats poolside.

3) Go out of your way to meet as many of your fellow uberettos as you can.

4) If you haven't figured it out yet, Miami's transportation sucks ass. #Slang as many Miamians, drivers, influencers as you can as passionately as you can and let them know why Uber will make this great city an even better place. Every slang matters. #MiamiNeedsUber . . .

5) If someone asks to meet the CEO and Founder of Uber, kindly introduce him to Max Crowley.

I don't think it's necessary for me to explain all that is wrong with this email. From its encouragement of immature fraternity-style partying to its cavalier reference to getting consent from a coworker for sex, it was initially shocking to me that this was okay at Uber for eight years, leading to the kind of culture former employees describe as toxic.

And It's Complicated

I have also learned that any substantive discourse on sexism is more complex. And it is far too easy to paint public figures as villains and heroes from looking at the surface. Here is the complicated truth. While the bone-headedness of this "party" email might be seared into the hard drive of the American public and women who take offense with its tone, and deservedly so, it is also true that one of Kalanick's first moves as CEO in 2011 was to hire Salle Yoo, a steely female partner from Davis Wright as Uber's general counsel. With Kalanick's support, Yoo quickly developed a reputation for a thoughtful progressive approach to ensuring gender equality in both workforce numbers and pay.

Yoo famously created a revolutionary formula at Uber for hiring a diverse workforce: (1) Hire women to senior positions. (2) Pay them the same as men.

Salle Yoo: **Fortune** *November 3, 2015*

> While I was working at the law firm Davis Wright Tremaine, the ABA Journal *published a story called "Early Exits," noting that nearly 100% of minority women lawyers leave their law firm within eight years. In other words, the probability that a minority woman associate would move up to partner was basically zero.*
>
> *This was 2006, and the story made me dig in my heels at my own firm and think, "I'm going to learn how to make partner and then teach other women how to advance."*
>
> *Well, I stayed at the law firm for 13 years, and yes, I made partner. And then, in 2012, I joined Uber as its first lawyer and employee No. 102. Over the past three years, as Uber's general counsel, I grew the legal team to over 120.*

My first five hires were women. I wasn't looking for women specifically. I set out to hire the best lawyers and legal team members to serve the needs of a quickly scaling company. I sought smart legal professionals who aligned with my vision that we would be partners in growth and who would thrive with the pace and pressure of a startup. As we've grown, my team has diversified, but one fact is notable: My female leads tend to build teams that are far more diverse, even beyond gender.

Being intentional about who you place at the top matters because of the flow-down effect. So it's ever critical who you put there.

I also take a data-driven approach in striving towards pay equity. Before any offer is made to a potential hire, I require that HR provide me with an updated chart that identifies compensation information for every hire in my department in the last year, by job level. This chart gives me the ability to double-check that men and women who have equivalent experience and are going into equivalent jobs receive equivalent salaries. Ensuring parity on the way is key; otherwise, the delta will simply grow over time.

Kalanick also brought on Rachel Whetstone from Google Ventures. I would argue that no traditionally "sexist" male CEO would bring in strong women like Yoo and Whetstone as part of core executive management team and allow them the independence to deliberately pursue diversity goals. In the researching of this book, I also learned Kalanick generously mentored female entrepreneurs. One of them, Melody McCloskey, CEO of StyleSeat, credits the Uber CEO with guiding her on how to successfully pitch all male VC's for funding money for her then fledgling company. And yet, as the very public news-making case of former Uber engineer Susan Fowler (whose superior retaliated when she refused to date him) makes crystal clear: the environment for female engineers became hostile and Uber failed to do its job as a company in supporting them.

I believe that the CEO should ultimately own company culture and employee morale (among other things). But the issue of Uber's culture appears far more complicated and nuanced than I first thought. I have learned an important lesson. I now argue that in order for us to have meaningful discourse about gender equality that derives real solutions, we need to move past headlines or personas and into systemic root causes and much more fundamental forces at play. Let's not simply rage against the bad guy. Let's instead rage against the machine.

The Bigger Picture

Uber's trials/struggles are symptomatic of occurrences at larger companies in other industries. So what about the bigger picture of what's going on in America today? For me, it's just as unbelievable that the Equal Rights Amendment has still not been ratified and women still earn 79 cents to every man's $1. In supposedly our most progressive segment of business, the tech sector, women represent fewer than 30 percent of the total workforce. This situation is even more abysmal in actual technical positions, where it is at a "high" of 17 percent at Google, and 10 percent at Twitter. Many are making courageous efforts to improve, but these numbers have been steadily declining since 1991, and we desperately need to figure out why.

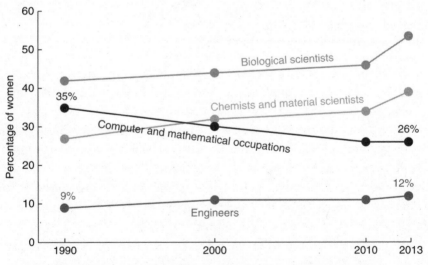

Women in selected STEM occupations, 1990–2013.

Sheryl Sandberg, the Facebook chief operating officer whose influential book *Lean In* offered a noble call to action that encouraged women to demand a seat at the table, take risks, and seek challenges, and asked men to realize the benefits of supporting women both in the workplace and at home, inspired many women and catalyzed a national conversation about gender equality. However, while "leaning in" was a necessary and brilliant step, it still accepts that women must advance *within* the current framework. I have a slight problem with this.

In 2015, software engineer Kate Heddleston, who attended Hackbright Academy's all-female computer coding course, remarked,

> Women in tech are the canary in the coal mine. Normally when the canary in the coal mine starts dying you know the environment is toxic and you should get out. Instead, the tech industry is looking at the canary, wondering why it can't breathe, saying "Lean in, canary. Lean in!" When one canary dies they get a new one because getting more canaries is how you fix the lack of canaries, right? Except the problem is that there isn't enough oxygen in the coal mine, not that there are too few canaries.

One Small Step for Womankind

As far as I'm concerned, it's time to do more than just ask women and men to lean in (that's a great first step). It's time to also give them the air they need to breathe. And so, in 2015, I decided to do my part by making a bold promise. I stated at an investor's conference that I would only invest in tech companies led by at least one female founder. I made this pledge because I believe that women make amazing entrepreneurs and leaders and that companies are simply better when there is a mix of both men and women. I did it because studies show that tech startups with at least one female founder hire twice as many women as companies with male-only founders. I did it because I wanted to help women get the most basic things they required to thrive and succeed.

While I knew the statement would be controversial, I was surprised at the vociferousness of the responses. From many women, I received a deluge of heartwarming expressions of thanks.

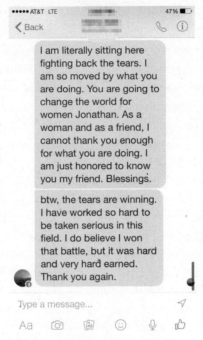

Text from a seasoned female executive.

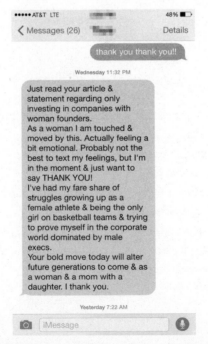

Text from another seasoned female executive.

There were lots of men who offered positive support as well. But from more men than I expected, I also received a preponderance of negative responses. I can divide their reactions up into four groups:

1. The "don't we live in a perfect meritocracy?" reaction:

john m. · 4 months ago
Most epic stupid idea ever. Stupid. Stupid. Stupid. Now even a low-performing woman could be hired just to meet the "quota" and get funded .Evolution and success will always be based on having the BEST people and ideas regardless of gender.
5 ∧ | ∨ · Reply · Share ›

plasmacutter ↱ Nick · 4 months ago
Spoken like someone who doesn't work in tech. My floor has 80 people, I'm one of 4 white men and the only non-minority on my team, except this is california, which became hispanic majority a few years ago, so where's my hegemonistic privilege? (technically, I'm jewish).

Our head of dev is a woman of color with 15 years in the field. Instead of crying about sexism and demanding preferential sexism, she worked hard as a coder and team player to become what she is today.
3 ∧ | ∨ · Reply · Share ›

2. The "it's obviously a pipeline problem" argument:

 plasmacutter ↱ COMMMONce...
9 hours ago

Even those who can code find themselves unsuited to high pressure environments and experience a lot of friction. We lean heavily female in our candidate screening for the sake of "diversity", yet only 1 in 10 applicants are female because very few women go into tech perido, and 90% of our female hires over the last 5 years have had an in-firm lifespan of 8 months or less.

0 ∧   ∨   Reply

3. The "I am a white male and fed up with being the bad guy" lament:

SuperiorWM
10 hours ago

White, straight, males comprise of about 5% of the global population but are apparently able to subjugate the rest of the globe... as we are blamed for the oppression of every other race and women. If that is true, maybe it is time to admit we just really are superior. Quite a feat for the 5%!

0 ∧   ∨   Reply

4. And my absolute favorite, "He must be a fag" comment. (Which I take as a compliment!)

TakesOnetoKnowOne · 4 months ago
He looks like a fruit.
∧ | ∨ · Reply · Share ›

It became clear to me that in order for us to change the system, we must catalyze these men to look at themselves and their own attitudes. Let's continue talking here.

Since it's still mostly men who invest and start companies (93 percent of VCs), manage employees (94.2 percent of CEOs), and sit on boards (80 percent of board seats), it goes to reason that it's men who are resisting change whether overtly or tacitly. It's us men who are metering the oxygen and causing the canaries to flee. And men, myself included, need to look hard at that.

When I returned to the United States at nine years old and reunited with my mom, she told me the greatest thing about this country was that anyone could be anything they wanted, as long as they worked hard, made good choices, and surrounded themselves with quality people. She instilled both an unfailing belief in myself and a confidence that the system was fair. I now realize this is true for only some of us. That's why today, I want to be a part of the worldwide effort to make gender equality in business a reality.

Night of the Living Bros

Walking into a steely high-rise in downtown San Francisco, Joyce and Katherine were very nervous. Nervous because heavy construction had made them horribly late. Nervous because they argued (like all startup founders do) over their pitch deck's numbers on estimated revenue. Nervous because Katherine's seven-year-old was sick at home, vomiting Cheerios under the care of a brand-new sitter. And, finally, nervous because they were meeting with one of the most successful venture capital firms in the country: they were kingmakers.

For any fledgling startup, a pitch meeting with this firm is like running the gauntlet; you have to present a perfectly reasoned argument with elegantly construed numbers around a sparklingly original business opportunity—and withstand an onslaught of detailed questions, data drill-downs, and razor-sharp critiques. But if you survive, you'll be awarded potentially millions in funding, access to top-quality talent to fill your startup's ranks, and the very best advice for growth.

Joyce and Katherine made their pitch with aplomb and alacrity. But they were first-time entrepreneurs who held nontechnical positions at their former companies, and their product targeted women. At the end of the session, Joyce ventured the critical question: "So what are our next steps?"

This is the moment when many women founders face a crushing blow: the recognition that their future success hangs by a thread from the subjective decisions of usually a group of men living in a men's world.

"This fashion category is not a category we're particularly interested in."

"We're sorry, but you don't have a technical cofounder, come back when you have a CTO."

"We like the idea, but we don't think you've got the . . . experience . . . to conquer the odds."

"It's a great pitch, but the product is for women. I'm going to have to go home and talk to my wife about it."

Joyce and Katherine never got their funding from any venture capital firm. Instead, they relied on an informal network of individual "angel" investors who funded their first round. I liked their idea very much, and I am proud to say I led their angel round.

Women Don't Get Funded

Right now, a paltry 7 percent of all technology companies that get funded are female-founded. The percentage of venture money going to female CEOs is just 3 percent.* This is true despite the fact that greater than half of all college graduates today are women and that, for STEM degrees in particular, the percentage of female graduates has been steadily approaching 50 percent over the past two decades. At the board level, women hold only 7.3 percent of all board seats in the U.S. tech industry.

To better understand why the business of venture capital and startups remains a bastion of white males, Canaan Partner's Maha Ibrahim explains that success in the game of funding startups is directly linked to "managing risk." In addition to a BA and PhD in economics, Ibrahim holds an MA in sociology from Stanford.

I'm going to equate starting a company to roulette. If I'm a venture investor, I get to have ten chips and I can set those ten chips on ten different numbers. If I'm a private company founder, I have one chip

---

*https://pando.com/2016/02/17/female-founder-raising-venture-capital-your-odds-are-even-worse-i-thought/.

and I'm playing roulette. That one chip means that I'm all in on one number. The risk is incredibly high. It's high personally, financially and professionally. I am sacrificing everything to make an idea work.

Ibrahim says managing risk for VCs and tech founders means staying in one's comfort zone and sticking with who and what you know:

These startups begin as small groups. They are small, homogenous groups for the most part because those founders are trying to eliminate risk. That small group similarity might be that they were all in the same engineering class at Stanford or that they're all in the same fraternity or they all have an e-commerce background.

Small groups tend to be homogeneous, and that's well understood in social. When somebody starts a private company with three other people or two other people, they look around for similarities. They look to control what they can control. People are trying to eliminate or minimize risk, and that, I think, is why most startups aren't very diverse.

Until they get to some number, maybe it's 15, maybe it's 20, maybe it's 30, where they actually have to start thinking about hiring for the best and the brightest as opposed to hiring for similarities and comfort.

In contrast, the Institute of Women's Policy Research (IWPR) has estimated that 30 percent of all businesses are owned by women.* While this statistic is heartening about the larger business landscape in the United States, it also serves to point up tech's shortcomings with regards to women. As an angel investor who hears pitches constantly, and as a CEO who creates gender-balanced teams, I see no shortage of highly qualified female candidates *every day*. I am fairly certain that there is no pipeline problem. If a company or team has a low female ratio, the problem is somewhere between the source and the end point.

According to a recent survey by Silicon Valley Bank, a leading provider of financial services to tech companies on the West Coast, nearly twice

---

*https://www.theatlantic.com/business/archive/2015/04/women-are-owning-more-and-more-small-businesses/390642/.

as many women (27 percent) said that the current fund-raising climate is "extremely challenging" versus male-founded companies. This same survey also found that 20 percent of female-founded companies were utterly unsuccessful raising money in 2016 versus only 13 percent of male ones. In the vast majority of the cases, the challenges are subtle, systemic, and the result of male-oriented pattern matching, like in the case of Joyce and Katherine. Sadly, in other instances, the challenges are harrowingly overt and more personal.

Getting Harassed Is Part of the Hustle

Chakira was born to be an entrepreneur. Growing up in Paris and of East Indian descent, she had the drive and the savoir-faire of an achiever. When she moved to Silicon Valley, she made quick work of getting to know key players, and soon enough, she was making great progress toward her life-long goal of becoming a successful founder and CEO. She led a crackerjack engineering team and was pitching her business plan to carefully targeted investors.

But on a cloudy Tuesday afternoon in Seattle, Chakira took a brief pause from her pitch and waxed gloomy about the prospects for her big data startup. When I asked how the fund-raising was going, she slowed and thought deliberately about her next words.

> I am just a little tired of having to always wear this fake wedding ring so guys I meet while pitching won't hit on me. It's hard enough as it is. It just adds that much more to deal with.

I was a little stunned. It was like watching a 30-year-old NBA all-star at the top of her game describing excruciating knee pain she'd been dealing with for years.

Soon after, I came across this post by my good friend Shauna Causey, another successful entrepreneur with multiple exits, who asked, on Facebook, "Have you ever faced sexual harassment at work?" Within a few hours, she received over 300 comments, with many answering, "Yes."

What's on your mind?

◉◀ Live   🖾 Photo   📍 Check In

f Good afternoon, Jonathan!

Shauna Causey
5 hrs · Palm Springs, CA · 🌐

Serious question. Just a simple yes or no... have you ever faced harassment at work (at any point in your career)? I'm curious how my friends would answer this question.

It feels like the recent news creates a safer space to admit publicly that it happens. Or even just admit it to ourselves. (Thank you, Susan Fowler and everyone else who has the courage to help us get to this point.)

👍😢😠 Diane Najm and 52 others   222 Comments

👍 Like   💬 Comment   ➤ Share

Vanessa Fox
Hahahahaha. It's funny because it's sad. It's sort of like asking if we've... See More

🗒   ▶   🛍   🌐   ≡

And as if on cue, later that day a former colleague with whom I worked at both Microsoft and Google, Niniane Wang, went public with her own story about sexual harassment at the hands of venture capitalist Justin Caldbeck, who had invested in her company:

Niniane Wang
Yesterday at 4:11 PM · 🌐

Justin Caldbeck harassed me in 2010, when he was a financial backer of my organization. By 2012, I knew of two other (Asian founder) women who he had harassed. (They are not Susan Ho nor Leiti Hsu.) I wracked my brain trying to come up with some way to warn other women. I even asked the founder of Change.org for suggestions. But it was always unclear what I could do. Women would tell me with resignation that they have gone through worse: "Yes, he pressured you for sex while he was your investor, but you didn't give in, so it could have been worse. When you tell people, it'll be he-said she-said, and he'll keep on doing it. This happens to women all the time."

For 7 years, I watched helplessly as Justin seemed to face no consequences for continuing to harass women pitching him for investment. His VC fund got bigger and bigger, and Justin seemed to get bolder and

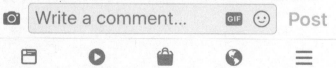

I could think of no parallels for men. While there are a few cases of men encountering unwanted advances, the vast majority of men in business simply don't have to deal with this additional overhead of interpreting the motives of a male colleague in a position of power. As the inspiring leader of LinkedIn, Reid Hoffman stated shortly after Niniane's story broke:

> VCs should understand that they have the same moral position to the entrepreneurs they interact with that a manager has to an employee, or a college professor to a student. That is to say, as soon as you start discussing potential business deals of any kind with an entrepreneur, there is no such thing as an innocent or appropriate sexual proposition or remark.*

Where does it start? Stanford law professor Michele Dauber recently told *Pando Daily*† that she repeatedly sees young women come to Stanford "full of hope and excitement about becoming entrepreneurs. And then some 43 percent of them endure some kind of sexual assault or misconduct and spend their freshman year grappling with that, while the men who deserve so many second chances spend their time networking in the tech world."‡

When massively valued tech companies can begin in garages and college dorms, we need to also take stock of what happens in those places and whether the system, from its very roots, supports and enables the behaviors we're seeing in the workplace.

The point is that men are still metering the oxygen in the room, and just a very, very few are causing it to stink. The vast majority of business leaders are good. But the key point here is that if you are a woman raising money, you not only have to deal with the baseline of "an extremely challenging" fund-raising environment, but occasionally deal with the extra credit "stuff." The decks are stacked indeed.

Under normal circumstances, the principal decision makers who hold the keys to the kingdom (VCs) are overwhelmingly male at 93 percent, and it is they who decide where and how these dollars are allocated. This is a

---

*Reid Hoffman, "The Human Rights of Women Entrepreneurs," *Medium,* June 23, 2017.
†Sarah Lacy, "The Valley Faced a Big Test in the Last Few Weeks. It Failed. What Now?" *Pando,* March 9, 2017.
‡Ibid.

male–female ratio among decision makers of 13 to 1. On corporate boards of Fortune 500 companies, the ratio is 5 to 1. And in the C-suite of these same companies? Also about 5 to 1. When the decision-making nexus is so overwhelmingly one-sided, women as the out-group don't get favorable results. Cause and effect. And when you add barriers such as those Chakira faced, it is nearly enough to make one give up. As Seattle venture capitalist Heather Redman wrote:

> [We] view the solution as much more systemic. It has to do with having **diverse teams at the highest levels of power** in our ecosystem. If Justin Caldbeck were an associate in his firm, he would not have harassed a partner. If Justin were a founder, he would not have harassed a woman VC from whom he was seeking funding. Justin would not have harassed a chief investment officer at one of his LPs. If Justin's other general partner had been a woman, he'd have been much less likely to harass any woman, even one subordinate to him in power.

The tech industry just happens to be the newest instance of this century-long problem in business as a whole. Fact is, no business sector in this country has gotten this completely right. Nationally it's not just that women earn less than men, they also earn less than men at every educational level and, in some cases, earn less than men who have lower qualifications at the same job. And in government, arguably where broad social priorities can be set, women still only compose about 20 percent of the legislature, 4 out of 50 state governors are women, and we still do not have a female president in the twenty-first century.

Even in industries where we assume women have near equal visibility, such as entertainment or music, the disparities are equally severe. When actor Natalie Portman starred in a 2011 film with male actor Ashton Kutcher, she had had more acting experience, higher international recognition, and a clear history of much bigger box office successes (*The Professional*, the Star Wars films, *Black Swan*) than her male costar. Yet Portman was paid just *one-third as much* as Kutcher. When their salaries were publicly disclosed, she said: "We just have a clear issue with women not having the same opportunities. **And men need to be part of the solution, not perpetuating the problem.**"

Portman makes a great point. Women have been speaking out powerfully and passionately for decades, but we seemed to have made incremental progress. The problem now lies in the fact that many men in positions of power haven't changed enough.

And, of course, I grant that it is hard to see the problem from the inside. I've been there myself. When you are part of the very framework that is causing an out-group to be disadvantaged, the dynamics are subtle and usually unintentional. From NAP.edu research on the four kinds of discrimination:

Vice President Pence ✓ 🐦 Follow
@VP

Appreciated joining @POTUS for meeting with the Freedom Caucus again today. This is it. #PassTheBill

11:21 AM - 23 Mar 2017

↩ 🔁 1,447   ♥ 5,627

Um . . . these are the people deciding our healthcare laws.

The main effect of subtle prejudice seems to be to favor the in-group rather than to directly disadvantage the out-group; in this sense, such prejudice is ambiguous rather than unambiguous. That is, the prejudice could indicate greater liking for the majority rather than greater disliking for the minority. As a practical matter, in a zero-sum setting, in-group advantage often results in the same outcome as out-group disadvantage but not always. Empirically, in-group members spontaneously reward the in-group, allocating discretionary resources to their own kind and thereby relatively disadvantaging the out-group (Brewer and Brown, 1998). People spontaneously view their own in-groups (but not the out-group) in a positive light, attributing its strengths to the essence of what makes a person part of the in-group (genes being a major example). The out-group's alleged defects are used to justify these behaviors. These ambiguous allocations and attributions constitute another subtle form of discrimination. (https://www.nap.edu/read/10887/chapter/7#58)

Men Must Be Part of the Solution

Surely, we can agree, as a broader business community, that we want better business results. We can also all agree as a society that gender equality is morally right. And if we are to make these great positive changes happen, the changes need to be joined and co-led by men. I strongly believe that men must now join in the change. Because it is still men who are metering the oxygen. Because it is still men who are currently still in control. And men in boardrooms are still the kingmakers who can ignite the fire to start great companies and dictate who else gets to be in the boardroom. Men like Travis Kalanick of Uber are the bosses and architects of company cultures, influencing what is acceptable workplace behavior. Men like Harvey Weinstein, Roger Ailes, and Bill O'Reilly victimize women with grave consequences to their work place cultures. Their companies are forever tarnished by having harbored these predators. And men like Donald Trump model behavior toward women to millions who admire him in the national spotlight and with the fixation of the media. If women are to get ahead, the agents who perpetuate sexism must stop. *Men must change, and men must take part in changing the broken parts of the system.* I invite all men out there to join me.

I think it is super important for men to be seen as gender advocates, because . . . 85 percent of our leaders are men . . . and if they are not gender advocates, then the culture won't change—we won't have the right environment. (National Center for Women in Technology, https://www .ncwit.org/resources/male-advocates-and-allies-promoting-gender-diversity-technology-workplaces)

And when we get this right, I know the benefits can be spectacular. As a direct result of gender-balanced teams that deeply understood their customer's desires and created brilliant products, several of my companies grew to achieve massive scale (up to 60 million unique users a month). My good friend Glenn Kelman's successful real estate company Redfin exhibited 25 percent year-over-year growth when the women in their workforce climbed from 10 percent to 35 percent. They recently IPO-ed in July 2017 at $1.73 billion. Another Seattle based tech giant Zillow recently received acknowledgment from *Fortune* magazine as one of the "Best Workplaces for Women," due to a very deep C-suite bench of senior leaders (both men and women) who have worked just as hard on gender and diversity goals as any conventional business objective. Frankly, I think the Seattle tech ecosystem will eventually lead the way on gender equality, and be a model for other tech hubs to follow.

And as we extend higher leadership positions to more women, the results are even more fantastic long term. Here are some facts that we need to make much more known:

- 80 women CEOs that the Boston research firm Quontopian followed during a 12-year study (2002–2014) were observed to produce equity returns for their shareholders of 226 percent better than the S&P 500 (http://fortune.com/2015/03/03/women-led-companies-perform-three-times-better-than-the-sp-500/).
- Credit Suisse found that companies with a female CEO had a return on equity averaging about 19 percent higher and dividend payouts about 9 percent higher than companies with a male CEO (https://www .cnbc.com/2016/09/25/female-ceos-board-members-super-charge-company-returns-credit-suisse-report.html).
- Companies with three or more women board members outperformed companies with zero women board members by 46 (return of equity) (www.catalyst.org/system/files/the_bottom_line_corporate_performance_and_women%27s_representation_on_boards_%282004-2008%29.pdf).
- A survey conducted by women.vc found that female general partners at venture firms outperformed the industry average at a 3.78x a net return

multiple. This is all the more impressive because women VCs are often segregated into areas that don't produce the highest returns; corporate VC groups, health care, and life sciences, or ecommerce where the largest "unicorn" valuations are rare (https://pando.com/2016/09/01/need-more-evidence-female-vcs-dont-lower-standards-industry-wide-female-partners-outperform-average/).

Frankly, I am shocked that more of these data points don't make bigger headlines. At the Aspen Institute, I once heard former Commander of Joint Special Operations Command General Stanley McChrystal speak of the need to channel much more research dollars into understanding newer, unexplored leadership styles that don't fit squarely into conventional profiles. I think he's onto something here, and I would suggest looking at women. I believe that advancing more women in the workplace and particularly in leadership is one way to unlock *new value* in corporate America.

Be a Change Master

Business consultant Ralph Bruksos famously wrote in his best seller *Turning Change into a Payday* that there are three distinct types of individuals in any revolution. I like his no-nonsense terminology, and with apologies to him, I will modify it to apply to three distinct profiles of men confronted with issues of gender equity in the workplace:

1. **Change Negatives.** These are people who deny change; they resist signals indicating that change is even necessary. On this issue of gender equality, these are men who are not only apathetic, but they don't understand why the issue matters. They may also believe that the world is already a meritocracy, or that in advocating for women we are actually guilty of reverse bias or reverse sexism. There is also fear that it's a zero-sum game, and there will be fewer opportunities for men if women are given more opportunity. These are the toughest cases. But even to this group, our solutions will apply if they only hear us.
2. **Change Neutrals.** They are those who neither help nor hinder. They go along for the ride. They are unwittingly in the bubble and agents of the ambiguous and unconscious prejudice described by the National Academies Press. But they can be a powerful force if you activate them. These men might simply have a lack of awareness, believe that the issue is just "too big," the rationale for change unclear, or lack time, given competing priorities.

I myself was a part of this group. I believe we have the most opportunity with this group. This group can be more easily activated with compelling arguments for change. And, finally, this group is numerically the biggest. Good people who simply don't know better.

3. **Change Masters.** Change masters are those who want change because they have had reasons derived from personal experience that change is necessary. They can be driven by moral obligation or mere business gain. They see opportunity in change.

   If you are reading this book, then you are already likely a *change master*. I invite you to be "patient zero" in your community or company and evangelize the ideas presented here.

   And according to the National Center for Women in Technology, the biggest factors influencing this change agent group are prior professional and personal experiences that have had some powerful influence on their thinking about gender issues. Typically, a combination of factors from both professional and personal realms activated them to be advocates.

Professional Experiences (91% of men)	Personal Experiences (83% of men)
Female Boss	Minority Experience
Learning about Microinequities	Working Wife/Partner
Aware Leaders	Daughter
Data Collection	Mother's or Sister's Experience
Seeing Gender Bias	Sense of Fairness

So how should we start? How should we create the necessary change? In the following chapters I will discuss eight practical solutions you can put to use in your own organization. If more companies adopt these proven tactics, we will be able to move the needle. They are:

Solution 1 Not enough women? How to look harder

Solution 2 In it to win it: Supporting women's development

Solution 3 Listen louder: Understand women's communication

Solution 4 Creating a family-forward culture

Solution 5 Just say no: High Performance Should Not Trump bad behavior

Solution 6 Adopt the ERA at your company

Solution 7 Stand together or fall apart

Solution 8 The future: Raising better men

Lisa Conquergood
Co-founder & CMO, PicMonkey. CMO, Knackshops.

Straight Talk: Be mindful of unintentionally discounting a woman's idea.

"I'd suggest watching for unintentionally ignoring or discounting a female colleague's idea. I've had female friends share stories, and I've witnessed this myself on many occasions where an idea is presented and it falls flat, only to have a male colleague say the same thing and it's suddenly an interesting idea! In a majority of cases, I do not believe it is intentional but it happens so often it would be comical if it weren't so frustrating."

2 | Solution 1: Not Enough Women? Look Harder

Look Harder Part A: Top of the Funnel

Washington is widely and proudly recognized as a progressive state that is home to progressive companies. Microsoft, the state's largest employer at roughly 114,000 employees, is a company that has pioneered some of the most forward-thinking corporate policies with regard to diversity and its fair treatment of women and minorities. And yet, as recently as 2015, only 17.1 percent of Microsoft's tech-related jobs and only 17.3 percent of its leadership positions were held by women. That same year, Dadaviz.com published a report that showed Seattle ranked dead last for the percentage of female tech company founders (8 percent) and female employees working for local tech firms (26 percent). Woah . . .

When even the most progressive companies in the most progressive states report such dismal numbers, it's time to dial 911. Clearly, there is an urgent need to do more. As Harvard Business School professor Bill George articulates in 7 *Lessons for Leading in Crisis*, the first step organizations must take in facing a crisis is to Face Reality Starting with Yourself. As a Washingtonian doing business there, I was shocked. The fact that only 24 female CEOs lead the top Fortune 500 companies in America means we definitely have a problem. The long-term health, growth, and sustainability of your company demands that managers *look harder* for qualified female candidates. Here are some meaningful solutions that will help you up your game.

What's in a Name? Anonymize Resumes

Source: iStock.

Numerous studies demonstrate that the lack of women and minorities in technology, management, and leadership positions has more to do with unconscious bias than any other factor. For example, a Cornell University report examined the question of whether redacting the names and addresses on resumes and reviewing them anonymously has an effect on how companies make hiring decisions:

> One of the [earlier] seminal studies on this topic looked at the effect that African American sounding names, e.g. Jamal and Lakisha, had on call back rates, finding that individuals with these names had 50% lower call back rates for interviews as compared to names typically associated with Caucasian individuals, e.g. Emily and Greg.1 . . . even when the quality of a given resume was taken into account. . . . **The findings are similar when resumes reveal information about gender** as opposed to race or ethnicity. A 2014 study focusing on scientists found that when evaluating resumes of a male and identically qualified female candidate, the evaluators rated the male applicant as more competent and employable. In addition, the participants in the study "selected a higher starting salary and offered more career mentoring to the male applicant.—Jeffrey Joseph, Cornell University, 2016[1]

Unconscious bias is rooted in preexisting social stereotypes and beliefs and can be so strong it can render a job candidate's proven skills and competitive attributes mute. These biases are usually the result of misguided socialization, random life experiences, and are unfortunately perpetuated in the media. People are loath to admit commonly shared biases, but associating all Asians with the math proficiency demonstrated by the two Korean whiz kids in your AP Calculus class is a prime example. It might lead one to conclude that Asian applicants are ideal candidates for technology or finance jobs. In that same vein, bearing witness to a female colleague tear up in anger, might lead to an assumption that all women have issues controlling their emotions in the workplace. Frankly, it's almost impossible to get rid of these unconscious biases.

Thankfully, managers *can* eliminate some unconscious bias at the top of the funnel, by addressing it at the point of candidate collection. In Victoria, Australia's most densely populated state, a leading-edge program called Recruit Smarter has already proven to work at scale. Created in 2016 by the Victorian government, the program was designed to test how recruiting bias might be eliminated by using software tools to anonymize job candidates' resumes. Employed by more than 30 large public- and private-sector organizations, including Deloitte, Ernst & Young, Dow Chemical, PricewaterhouseCoopers, Westpac, and the Victoria Police, Recruit Smarter removes bias-inducing details such as gender, cultural heritage, and age from resumes. Job candidates are no longer subject to the unconscious biases of those who are hiring. Even personal interests like yoga or dancing, which could suggest the candidate is a woman, are removed. The result? Participating companies actually experienced a measureable and significant increase in the number of women hired.

Similarly in England, Sweden, France, and Germany, removal of names, gender indicators, and backgrounds in reviewing resumes lead to more equal outcomes among groups within the very first phases of candidate selection.

Thus, for inclusion officers and diversity reps who have been tasked with ensuring a more diverse and robust workforce that better reflects the diversity of their customer base, methods like those used by the Recruit Smarter program are a straightforward solution to taking a significant step towards meeting diversity goals. If you run recruiting, please consider name blind resume review to remove bias. Several small and medium sized companies I know in Seattle have taken steps to create their own in-house tools to do the same thing, while others go old school and redact manually. Emerging new recruiting apps like Blendoor, Unitive, and GapJumpers are also viable solutions for redacting gender details. Any of these methods can move the needle!

Look Harder Part B: Minding the Gap

It's commonly known that when you're looking for a job, having a large gap on your resume is a red flag. According to the popular career advice blog, "Ask a Manager:"

> When employers see large gaps between jobs, they wonder what happened: Did you leave the previous job with nothing lined up, and if so, why? Were you fired? Did you blow up one day and walk off the job in a fit of rage? Were you working somewhere that you've deliberately left off your resume, and if so, are you trying to hide something that would be concerning if I knew about it? As for length, it's very unlikely that you'll ever even be asked about a gap of a few months or less. In general, gaps don't become a question for employers until they're five or six months or longer, and they don't become potential red flags until they're longer than that.

Of course, if you're a 22-year-old who took six months off after your internship at Merrill Lynch to island-hop in Thailand, your gap will likely not be a problem. However, if, at age 29, you left your senior-level project management position to give birth, raise kids, and at age 35 you want back in, you're most likely going to have a rough time of it. So much so that many of these women choose not even to try to reenter the workforce after having and raising their kids, even if they want to work and even if their family could use the extra income.

And so begins the great gender gap in pay, according to a new study published by Sari Kerr. According to the data, Kerr said, college-educated women make about 90 percent as much as men at age 25 and about 55 percent as much at age 45. The new working paper, which covered the broadest group of people over time, found that between ages 25 and 45, the gender pay gap for college graduates, which starts close to zero, widens by 55 percentage points. For those without college degrees, it widens by 28 percentage points.

Women who left high-paying occupations who were thriving as senior managers on the executive track report feeling discouraged and frustrated in their efforts to reenter the workforce at the level they left before having children. The act of having children and raising them has somehow rendered them "less than" in the workplace even though their management skill set remains as sharp and effective as the day they left.

If these women can somehow get in the door and have an interview at a company, they have a shot at explaining their situation and convincing the hiring manager to consider their experience and qualifications. However, existing ATS (applicant tracking software) tools are making it even harder for these women even to get their resumes looked at. Because the biggest and best companies receive huge volumes of applications every day, they are forced to rely on automated tools to filter the best candidates. Some of these tools look for time gaps, among other things. Time gaps are also flagged at the human level. Companies in the new economy are reluctant to hire returning new mothers because they mistakenly believe there will be a higher cost in both money and time to bring them up to speed on new systems and practices compared with candidates with no gap, that is, men. I think this must stop.

After being in a car accident with her daughter, Addie Swartz took some time off to help her daughter recover. As she considered her return to work, she witnessed the struggle of women like her trying to restart their careers. In an effort to solve this problem, Addie founded ReacHire, which works to help companies onboard returning women in innovative ways.

> Women that are coming back have strong life skills and have had to negotiate their way around a lot of things. They are used to compromising and navigating different situations and personalities. Anyone out more than two years needs to be updated, refreshed, because jobs are different and have more sophisticated systems. Technology changes significantly. But returning women are strong, thoughtful, capable professionals who can contribute greatly given the opportunity. — Addie Swartz, Inc. 2017[2]

Companies must lower the barriers to reentry and abandon their prejudices against women who want to have and care for their children. Instead, they need to see the personal experiences of these women as something positive and a value add to their products and services. Companies would benefit by tapping into this ready, willing, and eager talent pool, with the double benefit that we can again make significant improvements to gender equity at the *top* of the recruiting funnel.

And if you need further proof that looking into the gap can translate to real business value, I posit the experiences of my good friends Susan and Andrew Wright, founders of a fantastic consumer photos and print company in 2005 called SmileBox. Way advanced in their thinking about employee job sharing and the accommodation of working parents, Smile-Box had approximately one-third of its workforce composed of talented career women who took several gap years after leaving lucrative positions at larger companies. By being open minded in their hiring of reentering folks, and flexible in their structuring of in-office meeting times, they became one of the most prolific job providers of working parents in the Seattle tech ecosystem. I will never forget the glint in Andrew's eye when he divulged to me in 2011, "It's been the best thing. It's like this secret. This workforce is so talented and for some reason they have difficulty getting back into these larger companies. Susan and I are happy to give them a home here." It is no surprise that SmileBox, with its winning product line so reflecting of a gender-inclusive workforce, experienced double-digit revenue growth year over year, ultimately leading to a fantastic exit for the founders. It is still going strong today.

Part C: Stacking the Loop and Mining for Diamonds

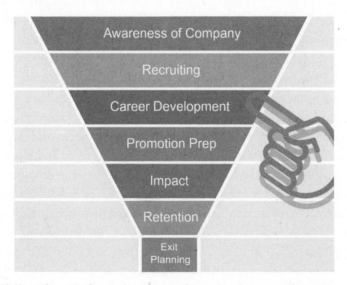

Middle of your funnel, where there is also much opportunity.

One of the best pieces of evidence that gender inequality in the workplace is not a pipeline problem but rather an issue of companies not putting in the necessary time and effort to find these women is a cool Seattle-based company called Redfin. Founded in 2004, Redfin is a residential real estate company that provides web-based database and brokerage services. Because it employs agents directly and gives them a salary, it avoids the commission-based system and instead ties compensation to customer satisfaction. Both homebuyers and sellers pay lower fees when they work or list with Redfin.

I first met Redfin's CEO Glenn Kelman, when he gave an emotionally charged and poignant keynote at Seattle 2.0, a then fringey conference designed specifically to celebrate the misfits, weirdos, and nut jobs who populated the burgeoning tech startup scene in Seattle during the early 2000s. It was geek "Lollapalooza." I loved the Seattle 2.0 conference so much that I eventually bought it for Geekwire and rebranded it "Geekwire Startup Day." But back in the early 2000s, being a tech entrepreneur was not an appetizing option for most smart tech workers. The dotcom crash was still fresh in people's minds, and if you were in Seattle working in tech, you wanted to be at a respectable company like Microsoft or Amazon, not a startup with only seven months' burn rate in reserves.

It is no surprise that as a disruptor and "misfit," Glenn is not only causing change in the real estate industry with his cutting-edge ideas, he's also revolutionizing how companies can tackle gender- and minority-based discrimination in the workplace. He is the type of "high-EQ" CEO who is as much about people as profits.

And in a great example of "better together," Kelman has teamed with an amazing CTO Bridget Frey, one of Redfin's first female engineers at their Seattle headquarters. Bridget is crisply well spoken, and my favorite advocate for more women in engineering. Together Frey and Kelman have taken the company's *technical* workforce to nearly 30 percent women.

Redfin proactively seeks out "nonwhite, nonmale" promotable individuals and sets specific and actionable diversity goals. According to Kelman and Frey, there are practical mechanisms that you can apply in your recruiting and hiring process, performance review cycles, and promotion key performance indicators (KPIs) to ensure you have a gender-balanced and diverse workforce.

For example, Frey believes keeping parents in the workforce with flexible schedules is key to improving diversity. She stresses that diversity is better for tech companies' bottom lines. As Frey noted in an interview with Geekwire:

> High-performing teams are teams that are able to get a lot of ideas on the table and then figure out what to do with those ideas . . . Having a diverse team is one way to manufacture that concept of having lots of ideas to choose from.—Bridget Frey, GeekWire.com, March 17, 2017

On gender equity, Bridget and Glenn are almost effusive to the degree of evangelism. They see the issue as both a moral imperative as well as a fundamentally strategic and competitive advantage for their company.

> "If you can attract more women, you can have a leg up on recruiting. Ties to real results!"
> "Don't you want to have a clear cultural differentiator to compete with the Googles and Facebooks?"
> "There is also arbitrage value to cornering an undervalued asset!"
> "We explicitly state that diversity is one of our top priorities, a priority that we consistently allocate resources to."

When they speak of three distinct ways that they "look harder," they offer the following.

Part D: Set Explicit Diversity Goals, Then Mirror Your Interview Loop to Match

Redfin didn't get to its enviable 30 percent women in technical positions overnight. It started with something highly controllable: insisting on a more diverse group of interviewers during the hiring process and using inherent social dynamics to their advantage. If you have goaled your technical division to have 30 percent women, then start by having a third of your *interviewers* be women.

The male selection bias that has worked against hiring and promoting women can actually be turned around to attract more women. The concept of affinity or similarity bias is where teams select others who share their own backgrounds or experiences. And while this is known to be one of the factors in why male-dominated fields sustain the exclusion of women, affinity bias can be turned around to favor women.

A 2015 study found there was greater gender parity on academic jour-nal editorial boards when the chief editor was high-performing, a younger professional and a woman (that is, 26% women on boards as compared to 16% under lower-performing and older male editors).[3]

> *These findings . . . suggest that younger professionals may be more used to working closely with female colleagues than older generations are. This leads them to be more likely to bypass the affinity bias, or even to see the female candidate as part of their in-group—regardless of gender."* —theconversation.com, 3/7/2017

Simply put, if you can get more woman participating in the interview process, you will hire more women. And this is exactly what Glenn and Bridget have done. When employees are selected for interview loops at Redfin, these days there are usually at least two female interviewers to a loop of five.

Some companies always have a woman in the room during every inter-view session. One of the companies I helmed, PicMonkey, has standard-ized the 2-on-1 interview for incoming candidates, where there is both a male and a female employee conducting the interview simultaneously. PicMonkey's head of HR, reports "having women as part of the interview process definitely helps to ensure that there isn't unconscious bias creep with regards to talent selection. Additionally, having clearly defined hiring crite-ria for interviewers to use while comparing potential hires also aids to ward off unconscious bias."

Here is the actual PicMonkey hiring loop for all incoming candidates:

- *Onsite interview:*
  - *1:1 with hiring manager*
  - *work challenge—hiring manager and sometimes senior peer*
  - *immediate work group interview—2 interviewers (1 male eng + **1 female eng**)*
  - *relational work group interview—2 interviewers (1 male eng + **1 female eng**)*
  - *portfolio review or technical interview if applicable (2–4, **mixed gender**)*

Now, this is a little controversial among some advocates of women in tech, with the main criticism being that many companies put token women in an interview loop who know little about the functional area the candidate is interviewing for. Don't do this. Don't put a marketing assistant on an engineering loop, and if you do, you *really* need to work on diversity at your company. A former Google colleague and accomplished author of best-selling *Cracking the Coding Interview*, Gayle Laakmann, advises:

> I actually think [adding women to interview loops] is fine most of the time . . . Don't drop a woman in there to talk to the candidate about how awesome it is to be a woman at your company; that will seem really disingenuous. Stick to business and don't make a big deal of the fact that the candidate is a woman.

> [Be careful that] some people see interviewing as an opportunity and others see it as a "punishment." Either way, you're offering an opportunity to one gender more than the other.

> You'll likely put a disproportionate recruiting burden on female employees. It's a zero sum game. If I'm interviewing more female candidates, then I'm interviewing more people total or I'm interviewing fewer men. Both are problems. It's not fair or ethical to tell women that, because of their gender, they need to do more recruiting activities.

All very fair points to consider. To remedy these problems, try the following:

- Identify women at your company whose passion for diversity is high and who will not view taking on interviewing as a burden.
- Ensure you match female interviewers with the same functional area as that of the job candidate, but allow for *adjacent* matches, too. If you're hiring an engineer, and have a large enough engineering work force, then of course put female *engineers* on the loop. But if you're too small, use adjacent matches. For an engineering loop, you can assign a female program manager or a female UX designer or a female test manager.
- Acknowledge cases where there's a disproportionate burden on female interviewers and compensate for it. I recommend giving them a comp day off for every sixth interview.

For those companies that are simply too small to field three female interviewers, how can you achieve lift off and not continue to perpetuate gender imbalance in hiring? I suggest that you *borrow your interviewers*. I can recall that back at both Microsoft and Google, division heads would routinely call in favors to borrow interviewers from another team. I believe informal networks of companies can do the same thing.

Here in Seattle, a number of male and female CEOs correspond on matters of hiring, funding, and general trends in the local marketplace. Sometimes we discuss how we feel about an out-of-town candidate interviewing at all of our companies, and the feeling is always collaborative rather than competitive. Two of the CEOs have even traded places for a month as an experiment on how leaders affect team cultures. I feel honored to have been invited into such a collegial and supportive cadre of leaders, and know that similar professional organizations either formal or informal exist everywhere. Once you develop decent calibration for the other leaders' hiring bar, it is an easy step to then ask to borrow interviewers on occasion. If you don't have enough female interviewers, ask to borrow some. Someone will pony up.

Part E: Pay Big Bonuses for Employee Referrals of Candidates from Underrepresented Backgrounds

The very best new employees at my companies come disproportionately as referrals from great existing employees. One afternoon, I decided to take stock of the best employees at one of my companies, with the original intent to see if some of the third-party recruiting agencies we had been utilizing over the last year were worth it. It shocked me that more than 80 percent of the list were referred from existing employees. It also gave me great data on who the "super referrers" were. Again, not surprisingly, the profile of the candidates mirrored the referrers. I got up on stage at the next all-hands meeting with an impassioned incentive: "I will *double* the existing referral bonus of $1,500 for any referral of female candidates who get hired."

As it turns out, I was a cheapskate. Intel recently announced that it would double its regular referral bonus (up to $4,000) for targeted diversity hires (i.e., underrepresented minorities, women, and veterans). And one of my favorite entrepreneurs and colleagues here in Seattle, Dan Shapiro, the founder of the highly successful Glowforge, offered a bonus exclusively for diversity hires (i.e., $5,000 for women, underrepresented minorities, or people with disabilities). Remarkable because most startups do not offer referral bonuses of any kind, let alone for minorities.

Do these bonuses actually work? Yes, they do. According to ERE Media, a national firm that provides online forums for human resources, talent acquisition, and recruiting professionals to network, share best practices, and learn from each other:

> By far, the most frequently asked question is "What single best practice has the most dramatic impact on diversity recruiting results?" Well without hesitation, our answer is . . .
>
> *"Focus your referral program on diversity and offer a significantly higher referral bonus for diversity hires."*

The diversity referral bonus has such a significant impact because it sends an unambiguous message about the importance of diversity recruiting. Corporations are constantly sending out messages to its employees about the value of diversity. Unfortunately, many employees and managers don't take those messages seriously because they often view them as "just talk." However, when you put your money where your mouth is by doubling the referral bonus, most will realize that corporate leadership is finally serious about diversity recruiting. So it's not just the money, but it's the public doubling of the amount that instantly lets your employees and managers unambiguously know how important diversity referrals have become.

Any of these individual diversity and inclusion initiatives can work significantly to meet your company's diversity goals. But according to the Kapor Center's research, having *all* of them implemented together will have a stronger impact than any one alone.

Part F: Mining for Diamonds and "Custom Grooming"

The team has gelled. Your product has launched. Now, you want to reward high performers and consider promotions. Senior leadership ranks may already be dominated by men, and you feel it's time to change the balance. But the hard truth is that promoting more women into the most senior leadership positions of your company may create new challenges for you.

These challenges sometimes come from shareholders and board members who are predominantly the "in group," who may not realize that they're in a bubble and practicing the forms of subtle, unconscious discrimination that we've described.

Even for other more successful entrepreneurs than I with a proven track record of success, the road to meaningful change isn't necessarily smooth.

A fellow CEO from Mountain View, California, recounted one experience where he was attempting to promote a star female employee. Her promotion was met with resistance by his then board, which heavily favored a man instead. Typically, the scenario is one where there is near parity between the male and female candidates, as well as:

- An apparent lack of confidence in the woman according to the all male board
- The woman's insistence on accuracy and erring conservatively on forecasts was misconstrued as "indecisiveness" or "lack of ambition"
- The favored male candidate had a prior connection to members of the board, whether from a previous company, business school, or social opportunities.

And I believe underlying all of this, are still perception issues around the traits classically attributed to "leaders" and how they differ from the traits that are traditionally ascribed to women. Berkshire Hathaway board member Charlotte Guyman (and a former boss whose leadership style I greatly admire) describes a necessary evolution in the way we must view professionalism and leadership that incorporates the classic "high success" attributes of *both* male and female. But until then, we all harbor unconscious biases.

Classic Male Attributes
- Courageous
- Aggressive
- Ambitious
- Willing to see and take risks
- Wanting to take control
- Results oriented
- Decisive
- Career first

Classic Female Attributes

- High integrity (honest, trustworthy) [both but often more aligned with females]
- Respectful to all levels of constituents (not just to the powerbrokers)
- Personally mature (no fits of anger or berating people or manipulation)
- Relationship oriented (seeks collaboration)
- Flexible leadership style
- Understands and can develop and utilize culture that also incorporates processes and rewarding teams, not just individuals
- Family first

Until we have evolved to define notions of great leadership as incorporating *both* lists of attributes, we're destined to unconsciously favor the status quo. Leaders like Glenn Kelman, Bridget Frey, and Charlotte Guyman represent a more evolved leadership style that successfully incorporates both lists.

And in the case of my friend's star female employee, she had exhibited all of the classically female traits in spades. Almost everyone who worked under her (men and women both) described her as "super capable," "the best manager they ever had," or "a person of highest integrity." She also exhibited many of the "male" traits as well, she *was* ambitious and courageous, but more quietly classy about it. Board members who couldn't possibly be able to interact with her with any real frequency at the company didn't see the value of this feedback from her direct reports. "We just don't see it" was the consistent answer to her advocates' efforts to communicate her efficacy. It was as if two different criteria were being used.

In the end, my friend did not succeed at overcoming his key shareholders' resistance and a much more traditionally defined "strong" male officer was promoted. This was demoralizing for many at the company who had felt the more qualified and capable candidate had lost. To me, this example underscores how difficult it can be to increase diversity among the executive ranks when there's a difference in how we value the attributes of women against men. We need to formalize how companies should increase diversity during promotions to executive ranks. But how?

Redfin has incorporated two key steps in its annual promotion cycles for the executive team. First, they ask, "How do we make sure the next 20 people we promote are not all white males? **Who are the top five people who are nonmale, nonwhite?**" That's it. Simple and elegant. But intentional and requiring commitment. Usually, this will yield a handful of folks added to the list whom all execs acknowledge are both capable and groomable.

The next step a company who is trying to be intentional about achieving racial or gender equity is something I call "custom grooming." As with grooming senior talent of any type, they ask:

"Does the employee **know** they're good at some things, but needs to work on other things to get ahead?"

It often involves taking a risk, making a bet on someone who does not fit the usual mold.

To best illustrate and underscore the importance of taking a risk and making a bet on somebody who is outside the norm, consider the evolution of venture capitalist and Carnegie Trustee Maha Ibrahim's career. Born of Egyptian heritage, devastatingly athletic, and raised as a brown-skinned girl in Boston, she was clearly not a card-carrying member of the men's club. Twenty years ago, as one of four females in a predominantly male PhD program in economics at MIT, Ibrahim says her career would not have been possible if a powerful mentor had not decided to take a risk by betting on her.

Decades later, that bet empowered Ibrahim to start her career as Canaan Partner's first female hire. Today 40 percent of Canaan Partner's investment team is female and three out of the eight general partners are women. Ibrahim has personally mentored a generation of female venture capitalists and entrepreneurs. To me, Canaan is another model for us all.

> My firm, we got here through osmosis. It was women hiring women. Everyone is going to hire people who are like them particularly in small group situations. You don't want people who rock the boat so you typically hire someone who has a similar background to you, maybe similar ethnicity, similar gender . . . whatever the similarity is, you're looking for that. My firm hired me and then hired women, not because I made it a cause for them to hire women but because I was comfortable hiring both men and women. So it's just one to get another to get another. We've reached a tipping point now where it's almost, and I hate to say this because it's such a new term, but it's almost a gender neutral environment.

Ibrahim is well known in tech circles as one of the most inclusive in terms of promoting racial and gender diversity. She says once she makes a hire or funds a startup she is "all in," which means engaging in active mentorship or "custom grooming" to ensure that individual's success.

Ibrahim's commitment to strong mentorship results from her own personal journey and a professor who she says took a big risk in mentoring her years ago.

I spent the mid-1990s in an economics PhD program at MIT. The program was comprised of an intense, diverse group of 28 grad students, four of them female (a ratio that mimics the tech world 20 years later). My senior thesis adviser was Professor Robert Solow, a Nobel Laureate and father of macroeconomics. Prior to meeting Professor Solow, I had been struggling to incorporate some brutally honest feedback from my original adviser, whose reaction to my first draft was completely ego-crushing. The only comment I recall from that feedback session was: "You write like a pig." Ouch!

The opportunity to work with Professor Solow was a true gift, particularly in light of the negative feedback received a few days earlier.

Professor Solow and I met monthly. He shared his wisdom with me that had come from decades of research in the field of economics. He guided me through my insecurities, wrong turns, mistakes, and successes. His advice to me was seldom specific to my thesis methodologies or the words or the numbers on the page. He was more a sideline coach, always urging me to keep my head up, be resilient, and keep charging.

When I graduated, Professor Solow allowed me to read a recommendation letter he had written on my behalf. His description of me was extremely generous and kind. What touched me the most, though, was the first sentence of his letter. He chose me to be the last graduate student in his incredibly successful, multidecade career as an economist. Several Nobel Prize winners and well-respected economists had studied under Professor Solow, and while I wasn't going to have their future careers in academia, he chose me and believed in me.

Fast-forward two decades. I am now a general partner at Canaan Partners. I've been fortunate to work alongside incredibly talented, intelligent, hardworking, high-integrity founders. I backed these founders, in part because of the markets they were going after, but also because I believed in them.

One such founder that I believe in wholeheartedly is Kevin Chou, CEO of Kabam. Like that of Professor Solow, my advice to Kevin is rarely specific to the business challenges he faces. We speak more about perseverance, risk tolerance, his team's capabilities, and the types of course corrections we can realistically make. Kevin knows his business far better than I ever will. I trust his instincts in directing the business. As his mentor, I am a sounding board for his concerns and, in many ways, a mirror for his self-confidence in times when he may doubt his capabilities.

Three pivots, five office moves, two name changes and a few near-death experiences later, the company is now one of the largest mobile gaming companies in the world. Kevin has led Kabam the entire way, setting the strategic direction while empowering his direct reports to execute in their own ways. He believes in his team the way I believe in him, the way Professor Solow believed in me.

Today, as a general partner, Ibrahim helps oversee a new $800 million Series A–focused fund and is recognized as one of the most successful VCs in the Bay Area. Twenty-five percent of Canaan's most recently funded companies were founded or cofounded by women. Compared to the industry-wide statistic, which puts venture investment in female-led startups at 3 percent, Canaan is clearly an outlier.

However, Ibrahim takes great pains to point out that she's not investing in specifically female-founded companies, she's looking for the best.

My job as a venture capitalist/investor is not to invest in a female founder and CEO, it's to make money and I am investing in a way that makes money. Venture people we're searching for data, we're searching for the best and at the same time we're trying to de-risk as much as we can in that search. But the concept of me investing in just women I think it's a fool's errand. Why? Because I have to invest in the best ideas and the best people. What that means is that it's inclusive of every demographic, every gender, every socioeconomic status, etc. Not bias towards one or another.

While Maha and I share the same goal of doing everything possible to nurture more diversity in business, investing exclusively in female-founded companies is one area where we agree to disagree. I think betting on investable, vetted women will turn out to be a higher return on investment long term, for the many reasons I have cited about women's leadership qualities. But where Maha and I are in complete agreement is the need for managers, boards, professors, and CEOs to *look harder*. Exceptional female candidates are there. There is no shortage of them.

Lisa Maki
CEO, Pokitdok

Straight Talk: "As a female founder, make sure you don't read too much into the 'female' connection when pitching to a woman VC and share more or give more time to them than you would to any other VC. They are no more nice, 'your friend,' or interested in helping you than any other VC. They are there to find great deals and make money for their LPs. Period."

3 | Solution 2: In It to Win It: Supporting Women's Development

Reverse Mentoring

hack[1]
/hak/ ◀))

1. a rough cut, blow, or stroke.
○ a tool for rough striking or cutting, e.g., a mattock or a miner's pick.

2. *informal*
an act of computer hacking.
○ a piece of computer code providing a quick or inelegant solution to a particular problem.
○ a strategy or technique for managing one's time or activities more efficiently.
○ "there's one easy hack to avoid alienating women at your company: try reverse mentoring"

When I invited Monica for lunch, I asked her to please pick a place she had never been but always wanted to try. "Ramen Man" was one of those tiny hole-in-the-wall places you sadly stop going to once you're out of your twenties, simply because you want good service.... But it was authentic, Japanese owned, and delicious in a way that makes you suspicious. Don't ask, don't tell . . .

Something in my gut was gnawing at me about Monica's impact on the GeekWire team, and I desperately wanted to engage face to face. My highly smart business partners John Cook and Todd Bishop wanted to give her more responsibility, but somehow my gut was saying no. Feedback from my business partners at GeekWire was that Monica had come from a prominent family in Malibu, raised in a household that was both bohemian, intellectual, and with Hollywood roots. Monica was self-assured for any age, incredibly hip, and opinionated. She also excelled at her job, distinguishing herself from peers much older through a consistent work ethic (gets to work by 7 a.m. every morning), smarts (able to learn every new software tool), and a winsome on-air presence (she occasionally hosted weekly podcasts for GeekWire). She was all of 23. Naturally, I hated her. But I also wanted to understand my company's investment in her and exactly *how* she was a force multiplier.

As we sat down over egg noodles, Monica spoke passionately about her teammates, and how she enjoyed their supportiveness to explore new content areas for GeekWire. She discussed opportunities for the business to extend to Millennials, offering a new podcast series called "Generation App," which eventually went on to be one of our most popular offerings. She also discussed the rabidly enthused, but younger segment of the tech community who can't afford our annual GW Summit or GW Awards ticket prices. Thus was born our return to smaller more casual meetups in more fringey venues. She spoke with zeal about the importance of pushing our editorial bounds further to make stories more compelling for girl geeks, a newly growing audience segment that encompassed an edgier and more subversive set. She discussed her own long-term ambitions in journalism and media and her commitment to evolving GeekWire. In short, she did all the things you are supposed to do when you have an audience with the chairman of the company, and in the process inoculated the very top of the organization with fresh, bold ideas. Boy, was I completely wrong about Monica. Always confident and assured, she even provided constructive feedback on how I could do better as a leader. She is the real deal.

And I had then realized that I could learn more from her than she could from me. I had just had my first "reverse mentoring" session.

Reverse mentoring is a formal concept first advanced by Alan Webber, the cofounder of Fast Company. "It's a situation where the old fogies in an organization realize that by the time you're in your forties and fifties, you're not in touch with the future the same way as the young twenty somethings. They come with fresh eyes, open minds, and instant links to the technology of our future."

Here are the five indisputable advantages of setting up a reverse mentoring program, where you pair a young woman with a senior man at your company:

- You send a super clear message that you value the voices of those who are not typically heard.
- You see with crystal clarity where your new leaders will emerge from.

- You gain a direct line of sight to issues all the way down the org. This is as close to being a sort of "undercover boss" as you can get.
- You close the chasm between generations: older employees learn about new apps, social media paradigms, or consumer behavior from a younger person and the younger person learns vital networking skills, business terminology, and industry practices from the older employee.

After my lunch with Monica, I realized that *I was part of the problem*. My initial reluctance to see her as a credible and long-term engine of future progress in our organization, when I certainly had no problem routinely lauding praises on one of her male colleagues of equal youthfulness, underscored my own hidden biases. To me, she always felt a little "lightweight," a bit "junior." But if you had pressed me for details, I wouldn't have been able to offer any substance behind those characterizations.

The second key epiphany was how much someone half my age could teach me. We are socialized to believe that "youth is wasted on the young," that the experience and wisdom we've accrued as we age remain relevant in perpetuity, and, thus, it is always a one-way conversation from old to young. But this simply isn't the case. It's bidirectional.

And according to a national leadership development company Catalyst for Action, in order for the reverse mentoring relationship to yield the highest gains, senior managers must commit intentionally to the following:

- Sincere willingness to learn: In a reverse mentoring relationship, both parties act in the capacity of a mentor as well as a mentee. And in order to switch roles so fluidly, both sides must genuinely *want* to learn from and share with the other.
- Trust: Reverse mentoring requires the trust of each party. The goal is to "push one another outside of their comfort zones and try new ways of thinking, working and being."
- Transparency: Both parties must be open with their feelings and with what they are thinking. They must be able to overcome differences in communication style (since different generations communicate differently) and be open to seeing situations from different angles.

So whatever became of Monica? She continues to be one of the stand-out stars of our organization. I have no doubt someday, she might run for president.

Monica getting top billing with veteran journalists.

Increasing Female Visibility

Koru CEO Kristen Hamilton receives the 2015 GeekWire "Startup of the Year" award.

All of a sudden, it starts drawing additional people . . . . So if other females see that person as a shining example and want to emulate them, they come in. They can draw talent both externally and internally. . . . So you do that on multiple fronts, and that can really, really help the organization grow from that overall diversity and global inclusion standpoint **without putting in place big diversity programs that need a lot of administrative care to keep moving**. —*Interview Subject, National Center for Women and Information Technology*

"Rebecca" is one of those phenomenal prodigies whom you admire and envy from the get-go. How she managed to graduate from college at age 19, then go directly to work at the New York office of JP Morgan is something that surely required a talent that few of us have at a young age. After a highly successful tenure at JP Morgan, she took a job on the opposite coast at one of my own alma maters: Microsoft. There, she was embedded in the corporate finance team, the "heartland" team, handling the entire company's profit and loss reporting to senior management, gaining insane amounts of visibility into which business succeeded or failed, and why. The fact that she had a direct line of mentorship with Microsoft's CFO was of incredible mutual benefit to the both of them. My guess is that, similar to my relationship with Monica, the more experienced CFO learned just as much from Rebecca as the reverse.

When Rebecca interviewed for the director of finance position at my company, I knew I had a secret weapon on my hands. I knew that beyond the scope of her job, Rebecca was the key to unlocking more women to becoming leaders at my company. Within two weeks of her starting, I began asking her to present as a regular at my weekly all-hands meetings to the entire company. While she was already winsome, articulate, and data-rich in her presentation style, She also asked me to mentor her to modulate presentations with humor, humanity, and humility.

And every week, she owned presenting the financial status of the company, usually a dry topic. As a profitable SAAS (or software as a service) company, there was always much to tell. Fluctuations in conversion rate from free users to pay . . . mix shifts between the monthly and yearly subscriptions . . . changes in final bill-through rate from one locale to the next . . . the take rate of a new product offering . . . we had to make these as interesting and fun to digest for the rest of the company as possible, so that folks stayed engaged and excited about their work. And Rebecca delivered beautifully.

From year 3 of PicMonkey, a typical all-hands meeting with the team. Always keep the meetings useful, entertaining, and mission-focused.

And as if on cue, something wonderful started to happen. One by one, other women at the company came forth to lead. Haley from operations asked to explore the finance area as a longer-term career option and to mentor under Rebecca. Samantha our administrative assistant also asked, "So what would be my steps in order to be like Rebecca some day?" Still others who were peers with Rebecca—Danielle who owned SEO/SEM, Kelly in program management, Crystal our design manager—began to take much more active and visible roles at company meetings. Our head of growth, Meredith, who was already on a parallel track of elevated visibility at the company, began to step up *her* game and her presentations became that much more engaging, peppering dry graphs and charts with colorful imagery from her hiking trips the prior weekend.

And after gaining more confidence in public speaking from the all-hands meetings, several of these folks extended their presentations to venues outside of the office, volunteering to speak at CFO conferences, marketing content seminars, meetups, and diversity inclusion events. Soon, our company developed a reputation in the ecosystem for having many women in critical positions, and women job candidates routinely applied in droves for any open position we had.

And this is something that's been corroborated in research. From the National Center for Women and Information Technology, who studied many companies and interviewed their leaders:

> Advocates observed that having diverse role models in leadership was important for the good of the company, for women's career development, for the success of recruitment and retention efforts, and for employee satisfaction and productivity . . . [they] believed that increasing the visibility of current female leaders was an important part of larger recruitment, retention, and advancement efforts. As one man observed, "More senior women in the leadership team will attract more females . . ."
>
> Increasing the visibility of female leaders and their achievements sends a message that females can be strong contributors and that they will be recognized and valued for their contributions. This strategy also is important because it is something that can begin almost immediately, whereas developing new female leaders may take more time.

Indeed, I have firsthand evidence that it is something that can begin almost immediately. And it works.

And when I apply these dynamics to a broader ecosystem, we can observe similar results. For decades many industry events sponsored by trade organizations and trade alliances were dominated by men, predominantly middle-aged, white, and suit clad. The typical speaker panel looked like this:

Oops, an all-male panel for a 2016 International Women's Day Conference in Melbourne Australia.
Source: Transdev Melbourne.

Then one day something hit me. I received this email from my good friend Stan Spiro, a well-known CEO in town. The email looked something like this:

Hey Guys,
    Someone on my team just asked me if GeekWire spends any effort balancing their speaker line up and panels with more women.
    If not, I urge you to do so. It makes a real difference. It's important.
    Stan

And I am embarrassed to admit that our first reaction was one of defensiveness. Hey, we have plenty of women on our panels! Why is he telling *us*? Who does he think it is? He's not the boss of us!!

GeekWire averages about 10 events every year, each one ranging from as few as 500 attendees for the more niche conferences (say our Sports Tech

Summit celebrating the intersection of sports and how technology advances athletes' performance and training) to our largest ones at 1,700 people (our annual GeekWire Ping Pong and Dodgeball tournament, or our Tech Summit). At each of these events, we typically have about 20 or so speakers and panelists. A fair estimate is that we ask about 170 to 200 people a year to take the stage.

But as a result of Stan's email, we did decide to take stock of our speaker lineup for the next upcoming event. And it did not look good. When we did the accounting, speaker after speaker, we saw a preponderance of men. Stan was right; we needed to do better.

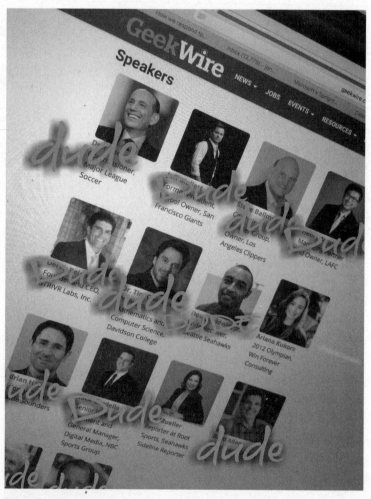

All really great male speakers, but we needed more women.

And as a result, we started to make some changes. Changes that would soon result in speaker lineups that reflected the world we wanted to live in. We goaled ourselves to be at an above par 35 percent female speakers. We started to lean on past female speakers to recommend additional women. Once we locked in the commitment from a few early speakers, wherever we had the option of a male or female speaker for the same slot, we would book the woman.

Our lineups then started to look more like the below. I am not saying we're always perfect, but we are getting better.

And soon after, just as offering more public visibility to female leaders at your company begets more female applicants, GeekWire saw a corresponding impact from more female representation on raising the sheer numbers of female attendees at these conferences. Our signals to the world that we were making a concerted effort to create more opportunities sent a clear message that we were in the business of creating inclusive environments.

2016 GeekWire Gala.

The Riveter cofounders Amy Nelson and Kim Peltola after winning the award for Newcomer of the Year.

CEO of Siren Susie Lee wins GeekWire's App of the Year (2016).

Yours truly fulfilling his duties as photobomber.

These attendees can't believe how gender noninclusive OTHER industry events are.

Eugenia Harvey
Owner of Kingdom Come Productions, PBS Series Producer
"Race Matters: Solutions"

Straight Talk: "Women have the same issues as African Americans. You have to be the very best to be taken seriously. In the words of my former boss 'You better walk on water.' And I thought, 'I see a lot of men around here drowning, so no problem.'"

Maria Hess
Head of Business Development, Growth & Marketing,
PicMonkey

Straight Talk: Being the default parent is distracting and challenging.

"It's not the case for every woman, but it does still seem to be the majority of mothers are the default parent, especially when both parents are working. Default parent means calls/texts during a meeting when little Johnny is sick, interruptions during the day for permission slips, doctor/dentist appointments, and so forth. Part of this is just life with kids. But part of the solution is setting up ways for businesses to be supportive and flexible, and not see this as a ding against performance or potential."

4 | Solution 3: Listen Louder

Much of the recent discussion about how to solve gender inequalities focuses on how to change women to sound more like men: to be more assertive, to pitch ideas with more of a "shoot for the stars" flair. I think that's backward. The long-term sustainable solution is not insisting that women change the way they speak, but that *men must learn to listen differently*.

Dragon Slayers and Deliberators

In 1982, Harvard psychologist Carol Gilligan published a landmark work on gender differences, *In a Different Voice*.[1] In this seminal work on the contrasting ways that men and women communicate, Gilligan discusses how the two sexes start to bifurcate at young ages in how they self-define, which in turn affects their communication style in adulthood. Boys begin defining themselves as "action men," slayers of dragons who pursue problems with aggression and conviction, often alone and using "I" words. Girls, in contrast, define themselves in terms of relationships with others and their constant linkage to those around them. Language used by women frequently uses inclusive pronouns such as "we" and "us." Men look at problems as math puzzles to be solved, while women work to ensure that lateral relationships remain strong and are not damaged.

Similarly, Tara Mohr, founder of the Playing Big leadership program for women, wrote:

> Listen with fresh ears to the women around you, and you'll hear some odd turns of phrase. You'll notice that much of the time their words sound like a kind of struggle—between saying something and holding back, between asserting and not being too assertive, between sharing an idea and diminishing it.[2]

Mohr presents a list of "little things" that women do in verbal communication—words and patterns that, to some, convey tentativeness, self-doubt, or self-deprecation:

- Just
- Actually
- Kind of
- Almost
- Sorry, but

- A little bit
- Speech patterns like uptalk

She asserts that female voices develop differently from girlhood, and that that needs to be okay. Rather than demanding that language be fast, immediate, and assertive, men need to learn to value deliberateness and even tentativeness. The care and caution that guides female language carry information. The burden should not solely be on the speaker but on the listener as well. As in all matters of human empathy, we must understand the signals before we judge.

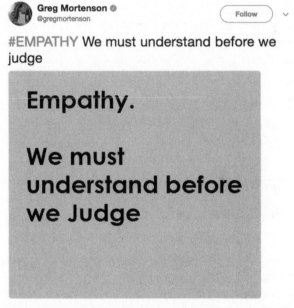

Greg Mortenson wrote *Three Cups of Tea*, a story about one man's mission to promote peace and to empower women in war-torn Afghanistan.

As with Charlotte Guyman's male/female leadership traits, we need not favor one over the other. A new kind of authentic and winning leadership needs to incorporate elements of both male and female leadership traits. Perhaps my former colleague Jennifer could have been better understood and appreciated for her deep talents if this kind of flexibility had been adopted.

Star Shooters and Stratosphere Blasters

Jennifer was one of the smartest and most results-driven professional that I had ever worked with during my time as an investor in a female-led startup: wicked smart, articulate, and winsome. In my book and according to her direct reports, Jenn demonstrated to us that she was a superstar with great leadership potential. In the eyes of her all-male investors, however, Jenn lacked confidence. No matter how hard she tried, the notion that she lacked confidence became a hurdle. During board meetings, Jennifer's answers to direct questions were always truthful and accurate, with detail and often appropriate qualifiers or the occasional caveat. She often presented projections that were more conservative. Her strategy, and one that is shared by many female executives, was to underpromise and then overdeliver. Jenn's communication style also had included a habit of pausing for clarification, asking, "Is this clear?" or "Am I missing anything?" Soliciting feedback and looking for reassurance that board members had their needs met ultimately served to her detriment. In my mind, there is no question that Jenn was an outstanding performer and a terrific leader. She had a 140 IQ, a track record of successes with multiple exits, 20 years of tech under her belt, and managed her family, which included two children. Jennifer's career had been highly successful at all levels prior to being a cofounder and entering the C-suite. But in her new role, the postmeeting feedback from the all-male investor group was filled with doubt and second guessing:

> "She seems hesitant, unsure."
> "I don't think she knows what she's talking about."
> "I don't think she's ready for this role."
> "She doesn't have enough experience."

This is an example of a phenomenon I call "women aim for the stratosphere, while men shoot for the stars."

The stark difference in business communication styles between men and women becomes profoundly magnified when it comes to the business of startups. Founders must be at their most persuasive and compelling best in pitch meetings with the venture capitalists. Often your pitch is honed down to just a few exciting slides communicating your company's vision, product roadmap, business model, risks, competitors, and a list of "soft circled" investors (those who've made a verbal commitment to invest). And even more importantly than visuals, your *verbal* communication must be compelling and confidence-inspiring. Most investors will say that they are really investing in the person more than they are the business. And you do all this within the first 10 to 15 minutes of a meeting regardless of its scheduled length. Startup incubators even streamline pitch times to just four minutes. As was the case with Joyce and Katherine, often you are pitching first to much more junior-level folks (almost always young men) where both life stage and communication gaps might be quite large.

Erika Trautman, a Yale- and Berkeley-educated broadcast journalist, left television in 2010 to start Rapt Media, a successful interactive video company with her husband. As one of only a handful of Colorado-based female founders, Trautman says the process of fund-raising is an unrelenting blur of grueling pitching and rejection. She estimates that, in order to secure the first million dollars of funding, she pitched over hundreds of times. In the business of startups, the CEO serves as the face of the company and the chief salesperson. Trautman watched and studied successful male founders and noted that their presentation style and oral promises took her out of her personal comfort zone.

> Male CEOs have a way of asserting future vision as if it were the present, without necessarily straight up lying. Although sometimes, they assert future vision as if it were true. I was told "You have to fund-raise with your confidence pants on." If you put forth something realistic, investors are going to cut it in half anyway. They think you're not shooting for the stars, but merely the stratosphere, and they don't like that.[3]

Erika says that taking a page from her male CEO peers, she attempted to play the game by making big and bold promises.

> I'm in a CEO group with a bunch of guys; I know how they are. One of the classic questions I encountered last year is how big do you think this opportunity can be, and you know that the right answer is a billion-dollar opportunity. I was told you better believe that at your core. You shouldn't go found a company that you think is going to be a 5-million-dollar opportunity. So during my next pitch, I said, "This is a billion-dollar opportunity," and I literally got laughed at. They were sort of like "Don't get ahead of yourself little lady"; that was the response I got.
>
> I think that with a guy they would have been like, "Well, he's a bit excessive, but I like his vision, I think he's aiming for the stars." I think that would have been well received because guys say it all the time. What I learned that works better was to say something like "I think this is an 895-million-dollar opportunity, and there's something about the specificity of that, that slows them down and

then they think maybe she's thought this through. What I think of the unconscious bias that I experience, and it makes sense to me, is *that men get jobs based on potential, women get jobs based on track record.*

I'm often told by female entrepreneurs that what seem to be subtle communication styles have large real-world consequences.

Identical Pitches Yield Biased Results

In a study commissioned by Harvard, Wharton, and MIT, investors who heard pitches by entrepreneurs preferred pitches by a man over the *identical* pitch from a woman twice as much (68 percent to 32 percent). According to this study:

> Male-narrated pitches were rated as more persuasive, logical and fact-based than were the same pitches narrated by a female voice.... To the extent that female entrepreneurs are disadvantaged in entrepreneurial pitching simply by virtue of their gender, then women may remain underrepresented in the entrepreneurial economy.[4]

Here's a graph published in the study illustrating the differences.

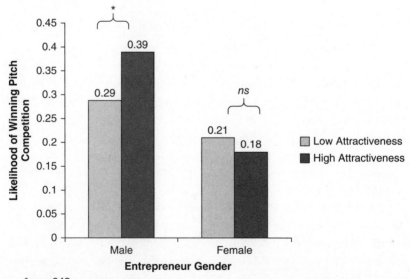

*$p = .042$

Incidentally, attractiveness, according to this graph, works as a double standard. While high attractiveness rewarded men with a 10-point boost for winning funding, it served as a detriment for women. It seems that if you're an attractive female entrepreneur who doesn't excel in bullshit, you're out of luck.

The study further points out that the gender imbalance in entrepreneurship is related to conventional and persistent differences between personality attributes ascribed to women versus those ascribed to entrepreneurs. Being an entrepreneur is equated with being bold, brash, a maverick—a slayer of dragons.

> Compared with men, women in male gender-typed positions are more likely to have their performance devalued, less likely to receive opportunities for career advancement, and more likely to encounter challenges and skepticism in starting and running ventures.

Furthermore, venture investors are always looking for the next *big* thing—not the next good thing or even the next successful thing.

Maha Ibrahim, the aforementioned champion and mentor of women in technology, has been funding female founders for 15 years as a most successful venture capitalist. Ibrahim observes on a regular basis how the perception by VCs that a woman's tendency to be measured and reasonable hurts them:

> We're looking for . . . the next Facebook. And in order to get that, we are looking for massive amounts of ambition, which sometimes people don't see in female founders. They do tend to reach for the moon and not the stars . . . There's some characteristic in female founders that is trying to take the most reasonable approach, not necessarily the most aggressive and ambitious approach.
>
> The bias is [the notion] that women are risk-averse [because] they are not showmen. A huge part of a male founder and CEO is that you are effectively the chief sales officer and chief marketing officer. You are the one spinning the massive vision, and that's what brings employees to you, potential acquirers to you. You are building something massive and huge and you can use every superlative you want. The perception and the bias is that the female entrepreneur is much more reasoned in their approach. They may want to get to the same place but . . . again as a stereotype, women tend to be more reasoned in their style.[5]

Ibrahim says this bias is as lethal to female entrepreneurs seeking funding as the notion that women cannot handle "hard" technology. Both are wrongheaded showstoppers.

There is a lot of energy around coaching women to *sound* more assertive, to speak with more *male* mannerisms in order to succeed in business. Tara Mohr has a well-intended checklist of things women can do to remove diminishing language from their business communication. These include checking for undermining disclaimers, places where points are hidden behind a question or unnecessary apologies, like "sorry to bother you." And from a highly recent Harvard Kennedy School study which included a review of U.S. Senate transcripts over 2 years, while men in positions of power tend to speak more in group settings, the researchers found that highly voluble (talkative) women were perceived by both males and females as *less* competent and less suitable for leadership. (*"Who Takes the Floor and Why"* – *Victoria Brescoll, Harvard Kennedy School.*)

So clearly, changing the way women talk to be more like men only solves half the problem while still excusing the legacy framework that is broken. We also need to solve the other side: *men must change how they listen.*

How Men Can Change the Way They Listen

1. **Don't confuse consensus building and inclusive language with weakness.** We must acknowledge that "diminishing" words occur naturally to women and are fundamentally rooted in the ways women develop language and self identify from childhood. They are not a reflection of character. Men should *not* view them reflexively as weakness or lack of conviction, but rather see them positively as bids for inclusion, collaborative problem solving, and allowance for multiple viewpoints in the workplace. They are meant to grease the skids, lower tension, and deepen work relationships. Next time you find yourself hearing a woman use these words, try not to focus on "weakness," but instead respond to her bid for your understanding and openness to her perspective.

2. **Don't confuse realism and a desire to deliver achievable results with lack of ambition.** Most women are not born bullshitters. What men might reflexively misconstrue as an unwillingness to aim high or a lack of aggressiveness to achieve the most spectacular results should

instead be viewed as sincere efforts to set clear expectations. As my female colleagues have often joked, "Women are just more realistic." Men should recognize that the data presented are the proverbial mid-line of the Monte Carlo curve, not the left outlying low likelihood curve. Again, this stems from the fundamental developmental differences between women and men. Relationships matter, and accuracy builds credibility.

3. **Practice active and empathetic listening skills.** These include micro-interactions that build the other person's self-esteem. To paraphrase Jack Zenger and Joself Folkman, founders of a leadership consultancy who wrote "What Great Listeners Actually Do" for the *Harvard Business Review*, the best listeners make the conversation a positive experience for the other side, which doesn't happen when the listener is passive or critical. Good listeners may challenge assumptions and disagree, but the person being listened to should feel that the listener is trying to help, not wanting to win an argument.[6]

Being a great listener in the workplace makes colleagues feel supported and creates a safe environment in which issues and differences can be discussed openly. This means not interrupting, not engaging in real-time debate, and not being eager to pounce and make your point. Most critically, being a great listener includes withholding your assumptions about the speaker's position.

Empathetic listeners withhold evaluation. This is one of the most important principles of learning, especially learning through the ear. This requires immense self-control. While listening, the main object is to comprehend each point made by the talker. Judgments and decisions (oh, such as lack of ambition or "weakness") should be suspended. After she has finished, review and assess her main ideas at face value.[7]

As Henry Ford said, "If there is any great secret of success in life, it lies in the ability to put oneself in another person's place and to see things from his or her point of view."

4. **Stop "mansplaining."** Coined by author Rebecca Solnit, mansplaining is when men explain something to a woman in a manner regarded as condescending or patronizing, usually starting with an assumption that the woman is less knowledgeable.

Solnit coined the term when she described in a *Los Angeles Times* essay how a man was explaining to her the arguments in her own book, without acknowledging that she wrote it. But mansplaining also has a more serious side. I know of at least two female colleagues who quit their jobs over the practice.[8]

Sweden's largest labor union, Unionen, famously staffed a "Mansplaining Hotline" in 2015 that fielded thousands of callers who phoned in during "mansplaining emergencies" to solicit tips on how to cope. However, the line quickly became dominated by angry male callers who talked at great length against the merits of such a line and, in turn, blocked many legitimate calls from women. To add insult to injury, female journalists who covered the issue were abused by male trolls on Twitter.

So why does this happen? Peter Tai Christensen, a gender expert at The Swedish Unionen, believes that mansplaining is an unconscious or conscious effort to restore male privilege at a time when traditional gender roles are perceived to be threatened.[9]

Mansplaining is maneuvering, tricks, and suppression techniques designed to put women "in their place," he said. He said whether it was intentional, a form of "misguided benevolence," or just a habit, "the problem is basically that women are assumed to be less knowing, competent, important, or legitimate."

> **Annemiek van Vleuten** @AvVleut... 5h
> I am now in the hospital with some injuries and fractures, but will be fine. Most of all super disappointed after best race of my career.
>
> ⟲ 3,643 ♥ 8,844
>
> ---
>
> **Martin A. Betancourt**
> @MartinArielB
>
> @AvVleuten first lesson in bicycling, keep your bike steady... whether fast or slow.
>
> 08/08/2016, 03:07
>
> **1 LIKE**
>
> ---
>
> **Roonil Wazlib**
> @beggie_smalls
>
> And today in 'Men on the Internet' this helpful guy mansplains cycling to an Olympic athlete
> 12:06 AM - 8 Aug 2016
> ↩ ⟲ 15,014 ♥ 20,607

Source: From Rachel Matthews, "The 9 Best Ways to Deal with Mansplaining at Work," *The Telegraph*, February 28, 2017, www.telegraph.co .uk/women/work/9-best-ways-deal-mansplaining-work/.

Men who find themselves mansplaining to a female colleague need to ask themselves these simple questions:

- Have you ever done her job?
- Have you seen her background work or due diligence?

- Have you been in service in that functional area more than she?
- Is your explanation relevant?
- Are you an expert?
- Did she ask?
- Are you her tutor, teacher, or person responsible for her education?
- Does she already know what you're about to say?

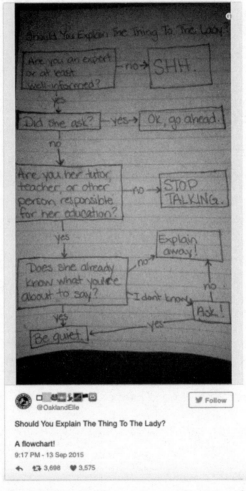

Should You Explain The Thing To The Lady?

A flowchart!
9:17 PM - 13 Sep 2015

↩ ⟲ 3,698 ♥ 3,575

Source: From Brandi Neal, "7 Ways to Respond to Mansplaining," *Bustle*, March 10, 2017, https://www.bustle.com/p/7-ways-to-respond-to-mansplaining-43514.

5. **Practice "turning toward" and getting curious.** The Seattle-based Gottman Institute is world famous for giving married couples practical exercises to strengthen their relationships. John and Julie Schwartz Gottman are noted psychologists known for their seminal work on marital stability and relationship analysis through direct scientific observations, many of which have been published in peer-reviewed literature.

To the surprise of many, I once used a company "all-hands" meeting to explain how I apply many of the Gottman principles to my relationships at work. Folks thought I was joking for the first minute and chuckled a little uncomfortably once they knew I was serious. Initially, my remarks were met with a lot of quizzical faces but I think most of us would agree that we spend our highest-quality thought cycles at the office versus at home. To me, applying mindful practices to ensure positive productive work relationships is a no-brainer. Two of my favorite Gottman exercises to apply in the workplace are "turn toward" and "get curious."

Turning toward is a powerful concept that stemmed from research that Dr. John Gottman did on thousands of couples. Years later he found that some were still together, while others had divorced. Those who stayed together intuitively practiced behavior that he coined "turning toward," which means they paid attention to bids for attention and correctly interpreted their subtext. A bid is an attempt to get affirmation, attention, or a connection. It can be in the form of a smile or a question for advice.

With a married couple, a bid might be, "How do I look?" and the subtext might be, "Will you please spend some time and attention on noticing me?"[10]

Gottman's research shows that men often miss these bids. Furthermore, they often misinterpret the subtext of the bid. I believe this same dynamic occurs in the workplace as well, whether the bid's source is male or female. Here are some examples of bids that I see happening in the workplace all the time, along with their subtext.

Text	Subtext
What's going on?	I want to learn more about what you're up to. If we're going to be working together, let's get to know each other.
Wanna get coffee?	Can I have your advice on what the heck just happened at the last meeting?
I talked to Joe today.	Will you chat with me about the org?
I had a terrible lunch meeting today.	Will you help me destress and tell me if I should be worried about my job?
I'm thinking of flying down to San Francisco for some meetings.	I'm a little worried about your division's status. Let's spend some face time together.

Turning toward is recognizing the bid and responding in a way that signals you understand the subtext. Sometimes that is as simple as saying, "Yes." Other times it is reflecting back your interpretation of what was asked, "Sounds like we should get to know each other!" If research proves that this skill causes married couples to stay together over decades simply because it makes people feel heard and understood, I think these same skills would do wonders in the workplace.

"Getting curious" is a companion idea that once you've heard a bid, you should explore the "why" of it. As author *Simon Sinek* famously said, "Everyone has a why. Why is the root purpose or belief that causes someone to do what they do." When you get curious about someone else's "why," you uncover the true reasons they believe what they are telling you and reinforce empathy listening.

The next time a female colleague states a forecast that seems "wrong" to you (too conservative, too high, etc.), get curious and practice asking a question that reveals what is hidden. Replace the brain impulse to judge with the desire to learn more. Ask:

"I'm curious to know how confident you feel about these numbers. And why?"

"I'm also curious to know how your level of confidence might change if the numbers were higher, or lower?"

And further: "What do I *not* know about your background analysis that might change how I look at this?"

Had Erika Trautman's investors practiced more turning toward, they might have at the very least followed up with thoughtful questions clarifying why Erika took a more conservative stance. If Jennifer's board members had gotten curious, they would have uncovered the incredible depth with which she had analyzed her forecast, and recalibrated their conclusions about her efficacy. Instead of only teaching women to talk differently, let's now train men to be better listeners.

Karen Cooper

Straight Talk: "It seems like men are praised when they leave work for a kid function, like 'Oh, what a great dad he is!' Whereas women are simply expected to do that. And in most of my personal experience and anecdotes from friends, it's often seen as negative. I've been coached not to say I'm leaving for a kid-related issue."

Susannah Malarkey
Lecturer in Finance, Foster School of Business,
University of Washington;
Former Executive Director, Technology Alliance

Straight Talk: "As a single mom running an organization I remember having to juggle things constantly and also just accepting that doing the best I could was all I could really ask of myself. But I could NEVER use motherhood as an excuse for missing anything at work. It was just not acceptable—not even when my child was sick. I remember the guilt I felt having to take my daughter as a toddler to 'sick kid' daycare because I had to be at the office. There is nothing worse for a mom than dropping a sick kid off for someone else to care for because you have to be at work. I never asked for any special consideration because I felt like I had to be as reliable, in fact more reliable, than any man. And I was. In fact, in retrospect I think I overachieved to prove that motherhood was something that would have zero impact on my work performance. Whether it was the weekends at the office working while my daughter watched videos or the early mornings and late nights of budget writing or editing or problem solving—I just did it. None of the men I was working with had a clue. All they knew was that I somehow managed to get it all done."

5

Solution 4: Creating a Family-Forward Culture

In 1997, I was a punk 29-year-old kid whose sole focus in life was work. I was single with no kids and had never heard of the phrase "work-life balance." In fact, I'm pretty sure the phrase had not yet been coined. And if it had, it had certainly not penetrated the hard Microsoft bubble, inside of which we were maniacally focused on our internal priorities and nothing else.

I will never forget what a jerk I made of myself one Halloween afternoon when the office closed "early" at 5:00 p.m. to allow families to trick-or-treat inside our building. The halls were wall to wall with employees from other divisions and their kids. I was already several years into my tenure in the attention-grabbing and fun Games Division, a division that others at the company viewed with a sort of disdain and fascination at the same time. Disdain because we were probably having way too much fun. Fascination because we were the strategic inroad into the living rooms of users. For Microsoft parents/employees from the heartland divisions of "Systems" or "Office," the games division became the obvious Halloween destination for family members.

Our hallways were adorned with dynamic and colorful marketing collateral: giant posters for games like Age of Empires, Starlancer, and

Mechwarrior. Nearly 75 percent of people's offices (mine included) sported action figure collections to rival any ComicCon vendor's booth. My own specialty was vintage robots from the 1970s, remnants from my own childhood that rooted me in a perpetual man-child state. I also happened to have classic coin-op games like Robotron, Defender, and Ms. Pac-Man right outside my door. Due to a fluke in seniority—the fluke being that most employees in the games division had been at the company less than three years—I had the corner office and direct access to the stairs leading to our brand-new cafeteria. The East Coast–bred writers from *Slate* housed upstairs would often come down to invite me to play games of Robotron (they were better than I by far). This basically meant that my office was the equivalent of Piazza San Marco in Venice, after the cruise ships have docked.

I was under deadline, working to create a presentation for the division's execs about the status of several games in production. One project in particular was not going well, and I was scrambling to figure out how to lower the bug count. Trouble was, I desperately needed to confer with my test manager who was across the building. Multiplayer capability across local area networks was still new and complex, and bug triages, rather than just once a week, were now a twice-daily occurrence. As I exited my office to another triage, I saw a giant kid-and-parent hoard closing in like a charging herd.

Source: Stock image.

In a flash, I was surrounded by screaming kids delighting in the bounty of candy and action figures. The irritation on my face was clear. As I worked upstream to round the turn to my test manager's office, I let out a loud "Ugh!" punctuated with the most emphatic eye roll. And when my eyes had rolled back, I saw the faces of my senior VP and his wife and kids. They heard me. I was mortified. I. Was. So. Fired. The punk up-and-comer had run smack into parents who were desperately trying to achieve their work-life balance, just a bit of a break to reconnect with their families.

My attitude was not uncommon. As my career developed further, I would notice how differently men and women handled the issue of work-life balance. While most of my male colleagues seemed to dawdle around the office into the evening, high VP level female managers like Lisa Brummel, Charlotte Guyman, and Patty Stonesifer would abruptly but politely end conversations, grab their bags around 5:15 p.m., and say, "Sorry, Jonathan. Let's pick up tomorrow. Gotta go!"

Their unapologetically straightforward signal to end the day in this way blew my 29 year old mind a little, and I learned to give myself permission to do the same to others years later when I became a parent and a CEO.

One day at a large E3 conference for games and entertainment software, the team I was traveling with decided to head out to dinner. A funny thing happens when teams do this: they don't always include the boss. One of my colleagues goaded me into asking my then boss, Charlotte, to join us for drinks and dinner out on the town. I will never forget Charlotte's polite but firm response.

Thanks but no thanks, Jonathan. Starting right now is some "Charlotte time" back at the hotel. I'll also be calling the kids.

A light bulb went off over my head. Yes, of course, family is more important than dinner with the coworkers. And while I was still in my twenties, unmarried and with no children, I carried this moment with me for years afterward.

During the height of World War II, Winston Churchill was asked if the government should defund the arts so that more money can be allocated to arms. He replied: *"Then what the hell are we fighting for?"*

Source: Getty Images.

I feel the same way about work-family balance. What is the purpose of work if we don't have time to spend with loved ones? When I was the CEO of PicMonkey, we advanced several highly practical "family-forward" sets of policies. I assert that in aggregate, these policies make a big difference in helping women succeed in the workplace. I will enumerate them here.

One: No Meetings before 9:00 a.m.

Email should not be about demonstrating effort and loyalty to the company. It's time that we drop conventional notions of what constitutes ambition and hard work and challenge antiquated ideas of what it is to be productive. In its most practical form, this is about alleviating the time pressure that working parents, *often the moms*, encounter every morning when juggling kids, school drop-off, and their own office readiness in the morning.

My Director of Operations at PicMonkey, who was in her 20s with no children, was clearly among the most capable executives on my team. In managing members of the operations team stationed in Dublin, she set daily meetings at 8:00 in the morning so that the Dublin team could join the call at 4:00 p.m. their time. The problem was that other execs, older working parents who had children, would miss out on something very important. My CRO at the time was a single mother of three, who being recently divorced was still figuring out the complex routine of shuttling kids across two households. While she was always the consummate professional and never complained, one morning near the coffee machine I explored, "So how are the kids this morning?" Her reply was truthful and effective: "I didn't see them. School doesn't start until 8:30 a.m., so I have my mom take them now."

I died a little when I heard this.

I started noticing that most of the other working moms (and some dads) at the office would arrive between 8:45 and 9:15 a.m., which is considered normal for tech. An informal poll showed almost all of these working moms, despite full-time jobs, shouldered the burden of childcare in the mornings. If their family didn't have a nanny or a grandparent, making a meeting at 8:00 a.m. was impossible. And if they did have childcare, they would attend the meeting but not see their kids.

From then on, at PicMonkey no meetings started before 9:00 a.m., to explicitly remove that trade-off working parents are often forced to make between time spent driving the kids to school versus making that morning meeting. Highly magnanimous in her accommodation of this change, the young Director of Operations understood the greater good and happily yielded on this issue. If you worked at PicMonkey and didn't see your kids in the morning, then that wasn't on us.

"Don't schedule leadership meetings after 5 p.m.," says Dr. Tejal Desai, professor and chair of Bioengineering and Therapeutic Sciences at University of California, San Francisco, who offers another easy solution to an issue that often becomes a wedge in the ascent of upwardly mobile, high-functioning female executives with children.

Widely recognized as one of the top scientists in the world, Dr. Desai directs the Laboratory of Therapeutic Micro and Nanotechnology at UCSF where her groundbreaking research involves micro- and nanofabrication techniques for drug delivery and tissue regeneration. This scientist who is saving lives and changing the world also happens to be the mother of three children. Despite being named to *Popular Science*'s Brilliant 10 and earning the National Science Foundation's CAREER award, which recognizes teacher-scholars most likely to become the academic leaders of the twenty-first century, Desai says irritatingly backward biases prevail.

A comment that I received from a senior male with a family of his own: "I can't believe you are having a third child. Your science is going to suffer." I stopped with a stunned look and just said, "Well, we'll see how it turns out." I wish I had a better comeback at that time, but eight years later I am one of two women chairs of a basic science department at UCSF, have a well-funded lab, and was elected to the National Academies. I guess it turned out okay and my science hasn't suffered too much!

In fact, the field of medicine and it's treatment of female physicians serves as another sobering proxy for the extreme difficulties working mothers face. A May 2017 UCSF survey found that Dr. Desai's experience is hardly out of the ordinary. In the survey, four out of five physician mothers reported discrimination, much of it based on motherhood. Of nearly 6,000 physician mothers surveyed by UCSF researchers, almost 78 percent reported discrimination of any type. Forms of perceived discrimination ranged from disrespect and reduced pay to being overlooked for promotions or being held to higher performance standards.

The study was published online by *JAMA Internal Medicine* on May 8, 2017. Previous research has shown that women physicians are typically paid lower salaries than male peers, are less likely to be promoted, and spend on average 8.5 more hours a week on household activities than male counterparts. The new research focused on how motherhood affects perceived discrimination among women physicians.

> Of those [6,000 female physicians surveyed], about 66 percent reported gender discrimination, while nearly 36 percent reported maternal discrimination. Approximately 32 percent reported discrimination based on pregnancy or maternity leave, and about 17 percent reported discrimination based on breastfeeding. Maternal discrimination was associated with higher burnout among the physician responders. Among the 2,070 female physicians reporting maternal discrimination, the most common forms were disrespectful treatment, not being included in administrative decision making, and pay or benefits not being equivalent to male peers.

Yet, much new research from neuroscientists are showing the very opposite of the above bias; when mammalian mothers are going through massive changes in their bodies as a result of pregnancy, that is when greater creativity and problem solving emerge. And while more research needs to be done with actual humans, cutting-edge research conducted in 2017 by professor of behavior neuroscience Kelly Lambert at the University of Richmond points to lab rat mothers being more inventive and resourceful post birth than their non-maternal counterparts, when given difficult food gathering and maze exercises. (from theatlantic.com Sept 12th 2017 "How Motherhood Affects Creativity") I think that in a similar way that General Stanley McChrystal advocates for new research on leadership to challenge legacy notions of what makes a successful leader, I believe we need to direct focus on the latest neuroscience to challenge traditional beliefs about motherhood and its impact on productivity. So far, the clearly observable neurological benefits from motherhood in lab rats seem to persist well past motherhood. Even after her offspring have long grown up, she will experience less memory decline in old age and continue to find new solutions to problems she had not considered before giving birth. In the very near future we should all be very excited, and probably not surprised, to find similar patterns with human mothers. Anecdotally, we all know of working parents who claim that they are much more efficient and task focused after being parents than before. Whether this is the result of learned behavior or changed physio-neurology will remain to be seen.

Point is, it appears that parenting is not the enemy of creative and meaningful work. So let's stop penalizing women for being parents!

Two: Men Should Take Just as Much Parental Leave as Women

It may seem odd that in the context of advancing women in corporate America, I assert that *men* should have the same parental leave benefits. Aren't we trying to help the women more here? But there are multiple reasons for this.

The first is the need to normalize the short-term, postbirth, reentry problem many women face. At some of the top companies in the United States, women typically get about five months off (three months of fully paid leave and another two months of partial pay), while the men get far less and are more likely to forgo the leave all together. In European countries such as Finland and the Netherlands, women are granted fully paid maternity leave up to a year while their job remains open upon their return, while the men typically take far less. And while catching up to European companies is something we should do, the larger problem is the significant difference between women's time away and men's.

After women have been gone from work for five months, they are often faced with:

- A sense that the work world has moved on, in terms of strategy, tactics, or organization
- A new marketplace and competition
- A sense that the job itself has changed
- Feeling "less than"
- Resentment from both men and childless women that they got to take a "sabbatical" with pay

On the other hand, men have none of those worries. For most men, if they take paternity leave, it's a "brief break." However, if more men were allowed to take the exact same amount of time off, they would become coworkers and bosses with a much greater appreciation for the reentry pressures that working mothers face. A blunt truth is that there are still today misguided attitudes in the workplace around mothers being "less than" when they come back, simply because they become coworkers who need to be brought up to speed on changes to the company or marketplace. But if men took just as much time off, supporting the onboarding of *all* reentering employees would simply become the default. And again, we might also build greater sympathy for colleagues.

Sarah, a former division head at a very large publicly traded software company, has a powerful personal anecdote that gets this point across:

One of the things that was a challenge for me was that I was one of the first parents at [the company] in the professional group. I worked for Hewlett-Packard for five years and I went back to business school and then I came to the company. So I was 30 when I started. Whereas, everybody else was about seven or eight years younger. And even the men who were around 30 really hadn't started having families yet.

It was subtle. So, for example, my first job out of business school I was in marketing, and I started in the spring, and I was pregnant in winter. That fall we did a huge program. They said everybody had to come in on Saturdays and do the call center, handle the phones, all day Saturday. I had a new baby, I had just come off maternity leave, and I just said I'm not going to do that. When my next review came around, I did not get more stock options. But I said I met all my goals, I've achieved everything, you just gave me a great review. And I heard, "You didn't come in on the days at the call center." That decision cost me a very huge and meaningful bonus.

Sarah advocates that parental leave policies just for women are not the solution. We need to make men take parental leave equally, too. Longer parental leave for men would have a powerful effect on men's role at home, with them taking on a greater share of the household chores. Evidence shows that there is a strong correlation between the equitable share of childrearing and the household burden and broader equity in society. Until men take parental leave and pick up "the second shift," we will always penalize women.

And I myself experienced firsthand the power of equal parental leave and its impact on my subsequent return. When I had my son in 2009, I was helming a company that I had cofounded, and traffic, headcount, and revenue were growing fast and furious. As hard as it was, I was fortunate to be able to take a lot of time off, starting on my wife's delivery date. I read a harrowing article about how new moms were 65 percent more likely to suffer postpartum depression if the husband was not helpful or absent, so I jumped into my parental leave with both feet. While that was probably still not enough (three years would have been best!), I dedicated myself to as much of the child-rearing duties as possible. Being at my wife's and baby's side 24/7, I learned the many ways in which raising a tiny human renders much of what I had previously taken for granted in the workplace nearly impossible. With sincere apologies to both women and men who have been seasoned "superparents" before this neophyte (including my mother the original superparent), here is a list of what I learned after my son was born:

- Sleep deprivation will knock out your memory and recall. Yes, there is such a thing as "baby brain." And man, did I lose focus at the office.
- Duh, it really is much easier to have two people to raise a child. This is not a Dan Quayle–era statement about traditional family values but a point about how raising a child while maintaining a full household is just easier when there is equal load balancing and real team work. For the first time, I felt like my wife and I were a team.
- The importance of being present and doing one thing at a time. You can't soothe a crying baby and check email at the same time. The email just needs to be less important.

- How you see other people with renewed eyes, when you realize that everyone was once a baby that someone took care of. That cantankerous jerk in marketing, he was once a cute baby. So maybe I can always find room in my heart to be kinder.
- How you see the kind of world that you want to create and live in, when you realize you will not always be around when your child grows old. Let's make this place better, not worse.

Upon my return to work, I became a *much* more sympathetic manager of working moms (and dads). I no longer counted a "debit" against a colleague if she couldn't recall a precise sales figure. I most certainly did not question commitment when a female colleague asked for time off when her child was sick. I stopped emailing or calling colleagues after normal work hours, which would obligate them to take their focus away from family. I no longer scheduled morale events outside of office hours. But most important, I started to *see* my female colleagues differently. I saw them as powerful multitaskers who efficiently dispensed with the day's tasks with alacrity and as capable leaders able to modulate tone and emotion to suit an irate child or a whiny adult with equal aplomb. Again, until men do their equal share and "pick up the second shift," they won't be able to truly appreciate what many working women go through.

Three: Shut Down Email at Night

Source: iStock.

I can remember being pregnant with my second one and it was Christmas Eve and I was at work trying to get everything straightened out. I had him at midnight Christmas Day, two minutes after midnight. [My CEO] was on email with me that day and I'm in labor. [The company] was very good to me. I'm not really complaining about the company, I'm just saying the substrate here. And the reason I ended up leaving running that big group, which was a fabulous job where I had hundreds of people working for me, was that I was pregnant with my third and I just thought I couldn't do this anymore. What would happen is on the weekend the management team, because I was at an executive level, would email, tons and tons of email, and make decisions that impacted my product group on the weekend. Well, okay, that's their right, but we have to think about that very carefully.
—Sarah, former division head of a publicly traded software company

One of the things that I love about email as a management tool is that it allows me to get tasks "off my chest" and into the queue of someone on my team. Ultimately, email, instant messaging, texting, and apps like Slack make us more productive. But there is a cost to all this connectivity: it puts working parents who are balancing their family lives at an utter disadvantage compared with childless employees.

Having created multiple businesses that scaled to serve tens of millions of users a month, I strongly believe that the majority of fundamental product and customer value is created with big, bold bets that happen in the first formative years of a business, and that these key decisions need to occur during normal business hours. Everything afterward, emails at night, chatter on Slack, extra comments in Google Docs, should merely be tools to augment the main event, and at best expected to provide marginal returns. Important to be sure, but as Warren Buffett famously said, "Superior market forces will beat or trump the actions of good or bad management." I'd like to posit a similar thought; "Superior work hour decisions will beat or trump good or bad off-hours emailing." If you've nailed your initial hypothesis about product/market fit or captured a sea change in user behavior during the work day, then everything thereafter is by definition an optimization, and eking out incremental gains. You make a more expensive trade than you think between productivity and employee morale if you create a company culture where much work occurs around the clock 24/7.

And if you're with me so far, then let's talk about employee productivity during the day. Research from the U.S. Bureau of Statistics on worker productivity reveals a startling disparity between hours spent at the office versus actual productivity. Overall, the research states that regardless of time logged behind a desk, the average knowledge worker is *productive about three hours per day.*

Three hours. Apparently, we are all spending time doing a lot of other things:

1. Reading news websites —1 hour 5 minutes
2. Checking social media—44 minutes
3. Discussing non-work-related things with coworkers—40 minutes
4. Searching for new jobs—26 minutes
5. Taking smoke breaks—23 minutes
6. Making calls to partners/friends—18 minutes
7. Making coffee—17 minutes
8. Texting or instant messaging—14 minutes
9. Eating snacks—8 minutes
10. Making food in office—7 minutes

Inc.com posited the following question:

> *"This research suggests that if you're productive for just 3 hours a day, you're outputting the same amount as someone in the office but for 8 hours. And imagine if we truly embraced this information. Even if we didn't cut a workday down to 3 hours, what if we cut it to 6? What if the norm was a workday of 11am–5pm?"*

I would thus argue that in an environment in which value creation is highly front loaded in a business's life cycle, and where ongoing employee productivity is three hours on average, then placing emphasis on after-hours emailing, weekend offsites, and early morning conference calls is of diminishing return. And as a boss, you normalize these behaviors of checking email around the clock for the whole team when you yourself send and respond to emails around the clock. If you do, that obligates others to do the same.

And the human cost to women and men with families is incredibly high.

I could remember after my divorce, on the weeks when I would have the two kids, there was always some drama in the evening. I only had the nanny during the day while I was at work, but when I would come home my focus was 300 percent on the children. But getting email questions with several colleagues and even at times board members would mean . . . I felt *compelled* to participate in the conversation. These other guys didn't care; they had their wives taking care of the kids while they clacked away all night. Other younger single employees would willingly jump on and you lived in constant angst of having entire conversations, with major decisions about the org or business, go on without you if you didn't jump in.
—Jennifer

For this reason I do three things:

1. I ceased all email activity from 6:00 p.m. to 8:00 a.m.
2. I asked that the entire company be off email at those hours to create an immediate standard of normative behavior.
3. I codified our company values to reflect this spirit of "work-life balance."

Here is an actual PicMonkey company value we codified in our review cycle for employees. I think the values highlighted with boldface sends a pretty clear message about our commitment to work-life balance:

At PicMonkey, we value highly team members who are:

- Collaborative, collegial, professional, and able to modulate emotions appropriate to their colleagues and business situation
- Intellectually rigorous, data-driven (both hard and soft data), pragmatically understanding causality, and striving for "why"
- Business-ambitious, oriented towards value creation, and impacting the bottom line for PicMonkey
- Courageous and willing to try new things, with low fear of failure
- Cross-exposed and "renaissance" in approach to problem solving, where the choices they make are informed by lessons from other business segments, user psychology, consumer sensibilities, the arts, or other applicable influences

- Work-life balanced: hard-working and highly efficient during conventional business hours, and able to maintain a healthy balance of activities outside of work
- Supportive of others' work-life balance: never applying pressure to colleagues, whether indirectly or directly, to take a hit in work-life balance

Four: Create Family-Friendly Spaces, Not Bro-Friendly Spaces

A lot of companies, particularly tech ones, pride themselves on progressivism in the area of office comforts. An arm's race has ensued for years since the days of Microsoft (All-you-can-drink soda!), through to Google (All-you-can-eat food from star restaurateur Charlie Ayers!!), Facebook (Nap rooms with futons! Sit really close to Mark Zuckerberg in the open space!!), and, finally, name-your-startup (beer fountains, beer pong, onsite masseuses, dry cleaning, valet parking . . .).

All-you-can-eat snacks, foosball, and yoga rooms seem great, but three months into a job, they become absolutely meaningless. Trust me, I know this. I've worked at Microsoft, been bought by Google twice, and roamed the halls of Facebook doing deals. And I thank them for all these perks. The secret is that all of these perks are designed to keep you at the office for as long as possible. I contend that far more meaningful office perks should instead focus on how to alleviate the burdens of an employee's life *outside* of work. To be truly meaningful to the *whole* employee, office perks should be provided to achieve work–life balance and to advance greater gender equity (not put working parents at a disadvantage). On your deathbed, no one will remember how many epic ping-pong games you played between the hours of 5:30 p.m. to 9 p.m. at the office.

At PicMonkey, one of the specific design goals for our office was to alleviate the logistical burdens of employees with children. Working with our architect, we allocated prime square footage of our office layout for families. Master architect Eric Cobb of cobbarch.com stated:

> While the obvious perks and amenities offered by an employer can be beneficial for a targeted user, a far more powerful impact is created through the design of smart, nonstandard spaces. If well conceived, unpredictable and unexpected spaces create an energetic atmosphere of creativity and flexibility. Without a prescribed "right way" to use these spaces, they encourage alternative uses and open the door for comfortable engagement, especially family friendly and without gender bias. Carefully building this commitment into the fabric of a work environment shapes the culture of an office.

We wanted to make our office kid-friendly so employees' children could be around anytime. We created a culture where kids weren't seen as a nuisance but a delight. We set out to design spaces where kids would actually enjoy being with their parents during the gap hours between school letting out and work being over.

A. We created the "living room" as a space where kids were encouraged to read, play with Legos, or watch their favorite parent-approved show.

**This should be 100 percent okay: the "living room."
PicMonkey program manager Kelly works while her son
hangs out for a few hours playing with test manager
Anthony's daughter.**

B. We enabled all meetings for video conferencing from home. Moore's law in the last five years has made video conferencing easy, fast, and cheap to enable. Google meeting requests have a default link where any meeting can become a video conference on your laptop. This is so easy, it's ludicrous.

And if you do this within an organization that has many families, you will see the "guilt cloud" disappear over the heads of the working parents in your employee pool. No longer will working moms be forced to make the occasional trade-off between tending to a sick child or being committed to work. Technology. Let's put it to work!

This should always be okay: New mom Jenn attends a meeting with her team while her son decides he won't go down for a nap.

Kids are always welcome. My son's school was canceled, and he spent the afternoon with me honing his photography skills.

C. Create in-office social time that is kid friendly. Most of the time morale events at offices are "happy hour"–style outings where colleagues bond over drinks. There's certainly nothing wrong with that. Bonding with coworkers is important. But I think most working parents who are overtaxed feel that if you're not going to be at the office working, then you might as well go home and be with family. So how about making these "happy hours" family friendly? I love hosting in-office parties where family and kids are invited because there are multiple benefits:

- Coworkers can bond with each other in a way that's "fuller spectrum" because they see the greater context from which a colleague comes (i.e., this person is both an outstanding engineer and an incredible parent).
- Families invited can in turn appreciate individuals in the workplace and perhaps the overall work culture, whom their family member has often talked about.
- Nothing is more disarming to uptight adults than cute kids.

     Thus, consider allocating room at your office for event spaces that can accommodate family-friendly morale events.

D. Dedicate space for new moms.

> The bathroom is great! I absolutely want to be nursing my new baby or pumping breast milk where people go to the bathroom!—said no one *ever*.
>
> Whatever good things we build, end up building us.—Jim Rohn

While space was fairly tight in our office, we knew we had expectant mothers among us and that group would probably continue to grow. In working with our architects, we invented private, configurable, and movable "cracker boxes" to provide safe spaces for mothers to nurse. We deliberately wrapped them to look like vintage "Graham Crackers" boxes, vintage toy packaging, and 1960s pop art, all to channel Warholian pop art themes related to consumer goods, as well as to explicitly reinforce themes of childhood, motherhood, and family.

This idea worked out so well for new mothers who needed privacy that we built some more.

Other successful, progressive companies have offered even better ideas:

Natalie Nagele, the cofounder of Philadelphia software company Wildbit, created a workspace that was also conceived from the get-go with her staff and their children in mind. Nagele says their mezzanine doubles as event space and a place for the kids to hang out. Parents can even hold parties there.

A 2015 Fast Company article profiled Wildbit and PicMonkey's family-friendly spaces. The reporter writes:

A working mother I know recently told me that toggling between parenting a toddler and the demands of managing a department and a staff of three is a tightrope walk. Some days, everything worked smoothly, boosting her confidence in her career path and her child-rearing choices. Other days, when her child got sick or daycare was closed due to weather, the disruption and reallocation of her time threatened to tip the fine balance between work and family. "It's stressful," she confesses. "It makes me feel like I'm not doing well at either job." What might help, she posits, is a more accepting environment. "One that doesn't punish you for having a life where things don't always run smoothly," she says.

Taking it to another level, Etsy, an online marketplace for small businesses based in San Francisco, has implemented the delightful concept of in-office "crafternoons," where parents and children can craft projects together. Appropriately, space in the office has been specially allocated to these regular activities. The combination of dedicated space and structured activities sponsored by the company sends clear messages that family time is valued. Not surprisingly, all these companies including PicMonkey also have generous family leave and vacation policies for all employees.

"Friends and family are always welcome to join employees during lunch, and we have high chairs in our kitchens to support and encourage family visits," Etsy company spokeswoman Ariana Anthony says.

Source: Fast Company.

Christina Watt
Former Senior Vice President of MWW Group, Founder of Exact Impact Coaching

Straight Talk: "In my experience, moms who are given flexible work situations will work harder than anyone else to prove themselves out of sheer appreciation. We need to get better at overcoming assumptions about how much or how hard working moms can or want to work. Moms going back to work are more efficient, more task oriented, and don't mess around. Talk to women—find out what flexibility they may want and need—and try not to make up stories about how your teams, organizations, or you, believe the work will go."

Dr. Tejal Desai
Chair and Professor of Bioengineering and Therapeutic Sciences at UCSF

Straight Talk: "Don't schedule 'leadership meetings' after 5 p.m. Don't assume just because a woman has kids that she doesn't want to take on more responsibility at work. A comment that I have gotten is, 'I can't believe you are having a third child. Your science is going to suffer.'"

6 | Solution 5: Just Say No: High Performance Should Not Trump Bad Behavior

Brie Larson after handing Casey Affleck the Oscar for Best Actor. Earlier, she had withheld clapping. Casey Affleck was accused of sexual harassment while on the set of *I'm Still Here* and settled out of court. Many, including Brie Larson, felt the Academy of Motion Picture Arts & Sciences turned a blind eye to this high performer when he was nominated later for *Manchester by the Sea*.

Source: Getty Images, Christopher Polk via Michelle Press.

Caught between a Rock and a Hard Place

Megan Ferguson knew she was destined to succeed in the tech industry someday. Oddly enough, growing up on a farm in rural eastern Oregon prepared her well for life in the big city. Coming from a large Catholic family of four kids, she was adept at giving flak to her brothers, all of whom were physically imposing boys who teased constantly and enjoyed making jokes about bodily functions. The kids routinely wrestled for the last scraps of dessert, muscled each other for prime space in front of the TV, and bested each other in footraces and pickup basketball games. Megan also spent a lot of time with her many aunts, who were loud and aggressive and proudly expressed their working-class values over beers and smokes at the local tavern. She grew up helping her dad burn the fields, chop down trees, and stack cords of firewood. Megan Ferguson was no delicate flower.

Megan also grew up to be the kind of woman men would find attractive. At 5 foot 7 and with a flair for style, Megan inspired her sister to ask: "When you go back to Silverton, do you sometimes feel like a supermodel?" Entering the sales division of a large tech company in San Francisco full of guys was in many ways familiar territory for Megan. Spending time with them at sales events or having dinners together came naturally to her, and even when they cajoled and teased, she felt like they were all just friends.

Then one day at a staff meeting of 20 of Megan's peers, her male boss said: "*I bet a girl like you is pretty kinky in bed.*"

There had been other inappropriate comments in the past, about her appearance or getting together in his hotel room while away on business. In fact, everyone already knew that this guy was sexist. Megan was put on his team in part because management felt that she could handle him. But this was the straw that broke the camel's back. She'd had it. "I don't even care about what he said, I just got tired of it," explained Megan. "Tired of having to sit in meetings with this guy wasting my time with talk like that."

After much fretting about what she should do, Megan contacted me to seek my professional opinion. I told her to file a formal complaint with HR so that she and the company could document this man's history of bad behavior. Her incredible performance with the company over the years would assuredly tip the scales in her favor, and her manager would be reprimanded. I also advised that she speak with the head of HR at my company, a professional whom I respected immensely and believed could provide an objective perspective on what constitutes a fireable offense, what remedies can be expected, and if she should lawyer up. After Megan had a highly productive meeting with my HR head, her confidence was bolstered. She met formally with the HR person at her own company, a generalist whose function was to oversee hiring, employee morale, and all other personnel matters.

Their response was: "Well, he *is* quite a high performer. So there's not a lot we can do."

This is not uncommon. Many small microaggressions get normalized, and an organization builds another substrate of tolerance for a sexist culture. When a female employee reaches her breaking point, she often worries about reporting the perpetrator, wondering if she's "being a prude" or if she should just let it slide because it's not worth the trouble. Most distressing for the victims of this sexual harassment is that they aren't sure whether their company will have their back if they tell their story. They understand that they could very well lose their job and compromise their career forever.

In many of these cases, high performance on the part of a harasser seem to trump rightful remedies. As managers, our reflex is to see these events as problems, a no-win scenario where you either have to fire the accused, who may be a legacy male high in the organization adding to the bottom line, or lose another employee of potentially equal impact to the organization, but usually more junior and earning less by virtue of being a woman. Too often, overburdened managers will favor the short-term gain over the long.

How Long Has This Been Happening?

In the fall of 1991, networks broadcast live gavel-to-gavel coverage of the confirmation hearing of Supreme Court nominee Judge Clarence Thomas. That October, the country witnessed an articulate and composed 35-year-old law professor, Anita Hill, give riveting testimony under oath before the Senate Judiciary alleging that Judge Thomas had repeatedly subjected her to harassment. For working women of a certain age, the details were lurid, but the circumstances felt all-too familiar.

In daring to publicly voice the insulting behaviors and unwanted overtures that she endured from her former boss, Anita Hill immediately found herself under attack by some disbelieving and openly hostile members of the all-white male committee. The insults included one disbelieving senior senator who theorized that Hill suffered from a psychiatric condition where a woman fantasizes that a powerful man is in love with her.

She was also attacked by many in the African American community who saw her challenge of a fellow African American's right to serve on the country's highest court as sabotage. For working women, who had long endured unwanted physical contact by superiors or hostile, demeaning gestures and verbal abuse by male colleagues, the hearings marked a watershed moment. Even though Judge Thomas's appointment prevailed, Hill's courage and unflappable resolve inspired national discussion about workplace behaviors and fomented a movement for companies to enact formal workplace policies.

Fast forward to June 23, 2017. Dateline: Silicon Valley, California, aka the West Coast vortex of mass wealth and power. Like the Clarence Thomas hearings of the 1990s, this date will likely be long remembered as a turning point for sexual harassment and women in tech. My own former colleague and longtime friend, Niniane Wang, plays the role of the twenty-first-century version of Anita Hill.

It is the evening after the *Information* published a potentially career-crushing story about a white married male venture capitalist who had used money from the $300 million fund he managed as an excuse to pressure female founders for sex. Evertoon CEO Niniane Wang, who had publicly outed investor Justin Caldbeck, says she had taken great personal and professional risk in speaking out about her experience with the Binary Capital cofounder. Wang had also convinced two other female CEOs to go on the record with her. While I found Niniane's bravery extraordinary and thus I quote the details here, I also believe that it's important for others who are also considering coming forth to understand what the life cycle of calling out sexual harassment can feel like:

> After the article came out . . . And so we've spent all this work for the article to come out and for eight hours almost no one talked about it or tweeted it. There was no buzz at all. There was one article from Sarah Lacy but that was it. And so I really thought that we had failed. And I had convinced the two other women to go on the record with me. They came to my house for three and a half hours—or one of them to my house and I convinced her over dinner to do it. And so when it looked like it had failed she said to me it was her worst fear. That she had used her name and

yet we had no impact. And when she said that, my stomach sank. Because I felt like I was trying to protect women and instead I've hurt two women who put their careers on the line and we had received nothing. And now it might be harder for them to fund-raise. And I felt like I had actually damaged these women. So it was horrible.

In the face of potentially catastrophic outcomes, Wang turned to friend and investor, Ellen Pao. Some five years ago Ellen Pao lost her famous sexual harassment case against her former partners at all-powerful Kleiner Perkins. Meanwhile, Caldbeck had issued a flat denial and had threatened to personally sue the reporter.

Justin had sent the text to the reporter saying our lawyers will be in touch. So we had spent all this work and everything—and everybody was going to suffer. And then I messaged Ellen Pao and she said, "No, you were very brave." And I said, "Yea, but it didn't work. Nothing's happening." And she said "You know what, I'm going to help." And I said, "Oh you don't have to, but you know, if you want to, great."

Pao reassured Wang that the year she had dedicated to working on the story would not be lost. She began tweeting and retweeting about the article and support for the small cadre of Asian American CEOs.

And then she (Pao) spent hours that night retweeting every VC who tweeted about it. And then that generated more and more attention. And some of those people like you know had maybe not supported her in the past. And so I felt like she really rose above any of her own personal feelings about who had supported her, not supported her. But she did what was right for this situation. And people even told me like some of those people she was helping, they had kind of wronged her in the past. But she still did it.

Wang says Pao's support and perseverance paid off when much-respected and revered male venture capitalists like angel investor David Hornik and Reid Hoffman of Greylock Partners began retweeting the article and expressing support for the women. Hoffman went further and asked men to take the "Decency Pledge" and called for a change in the work conditions for female colleagues.

Reid Hoffman

Former CEO of LinkedIn and Silicon Valley luminary Reid Hoffman took a stand just days later to articulate that VCs must hold the same moral position to entrepreneurs as manager/employee or professor/student. In a piece published on LinkedIn titled "The Human Rights of Women Entrepreneurs," Hoffman urged his colleagues in the venture capital industry to stand up whenever they see a fellow VC behave inappropriately.

Two days after Hoffman and other major domos in the industry chimed in, Caldbeck announced an "indefinite leave" from the firm. Wang says Silicon Valley heavyweights who chimed in were instrumental in removing a serial predator and would save future women from being victimized.

> You know, Reid Hoffman wrote this post which then got tweeted. I think it would have died without the help of all these people. Without all these people who rose up and helped. Eventually once it got enough attention, it got a life of its own. Sarah Lacy personally called out a lot of VCs and asked them to support. So I think a lot of people really tried to help.

The public revelations about Justin Caldbeck's predatory behavior sent a collective shudder through the community. But the women of Bay Area tech companies say they were hardly surprised. In the small circle of successful female-led startups, Caldbeck's behavior had circulated for years at his previous firm of Lightspeed Capital and while at Bain. The Binary story proved to be a tipping point on the issue of sexual harassment in the tech industry. Within a matter of weeks a handful of powerful figures in venture capital in San Francisco and Seattle would resign their posts for similar bad behaviors.

In early July 2017, one by one, female entrepreneurs started outing men who touched, groped, kissed, and propositioned them. These men ran bigger, more substantial funds, sat on numerous boards, and were much more popular figures than Caldbeck. Women who had come to them as professionals seeking funding for their companies were instead propositioned for sex.

The takeaway from the Binary story is the fact that Caldbeck's bad behavior reportedly dated back to his days at Bain and Lightspeed Capital. The revelation that the board of Lightspeed Capital had been informed about predatory behavior led people to wonder why he had been allowed to continue work unabated. The revelations that STITCHFIX CEO Katrina Lake had Caldbeck fired from her board after she experienced an unwanted advance left women in the Valley shaking their heads.

Simply put, Caldbeck was allowed to carry on because, ostensibly, he was "adding value" and also because others around him ignored the problem.

The Cost of Ignoring the Problem

If you do look at the long term, you'll find that there's a huge cost to turning a blind eye to the misbehaving high performer. While the Justin Caldbeck scenario is most severe in magnitude, it is unfortunately very common for women in industry to receive unwanted sexual attention. For the tech industry alone, that cost is estimated to be $16 billion a year, according to a first-of-its-kind "Leavers Study" from the Kapor Center for Social Impact. Exploring the relationship between workplace culture and why people leave a job, this cross-sectional study aggregated the sum total replacement cost of losing women (inclusive of minority women) who leave due to being treated unfairly in the workplace, inclusive of sexual harassment.

Financial Costs of Turnover Due to Unfairness/Mistreatment

Race/Ethnicity	% of 2016 Computing Workforce	# of 2016 Computing Workforce	# Leaving Due to Voluntary Turnover (6.15%)	Turnover Rate Due to Unfairness	# Leaving Due to Unfairness	Cost for Making an Engineering Hire ($17,000)	Full Replacement Costs at 1.5x Average Salary ($144,834.24)
White	70%	3,483,900	214,260	35%	74,991		
Asian	18%	895,860	55,095	44%	24,242		
Black	8%	398,160	24,487	34%	8,326		
Other	4%	199,080	12,243	34%	4,163		
Latinx (of any race)	7%						
Total			4,977,000	306,085	37%	111,722	$1,899,274,000	$16,181,170,961

Source: Kapor Center (Kim Bardakian).

While the study also uncovered other issues of unfairness women face in the workplace in addition to sexual harassment, I felt it germane to our discussion to include the full findings. Among a large sample of more than 2,000 people who had recently quit their jobs:

- Women had significantly more experiences with unfair treatment than men.

- One in 10 women reported experiencing unwanted sexual attention; 55 percent of them said this experience definitely influenced their decision to leave a company.
- Of those women who experienced unwanted sexual attention, 56 percent said these types of experiences also contributed to their decision to leave their *previous* job.
- Women reported others taking credit for their work (27 percent), being passed over for a promotion (25 percent), and assumptions about their ability (16 percent) at rates higher than men (22, 22, and 13 percent).
- Women of color reported the highest rates of being passed over for promotion (30 percent), being stereotyped (24 percent), and having their identity mistaken for another person of the same race/gender (17 percent) of any group.
- More than a third (35 percent) of former employees said their experiences would make them less likely to refer others to seek a job at their former employer, and a quarter (25 percent) said they would be less likely to recommend others to buy or use products and services from their former employer.

The bottom line: unfairness for women in the workplace, with sexual harassment being a key issue, is sadly happening more prevalently than we think, and the cost to doing nothing has real economic impact on us.

So what can you do as a company leader to prevent women from leaving for these reasons? Currently, there are several workplace initiatives that together seem to be working. Each one alone helps but it is the totality of them that creates a multiplying effect on culture.

D&I: Hire a Diversity and Inclusion Director

Believe me, I've been the CEO who tried to do diversity and inclusiveness efforts part time, and it's not easy. While I thought consistent messaging about the importance of gender and diversity inclusion at all-hands meetings was a big deal, I realized I had still failed when one afternoon I was told that several women at the company were comparing notes and lamenting how they perceived potentially dwindling advancement opportunities, triggered by having been talked down to by a male manager during a particularly tense bug committee meeting. While spoken words from the top affirm cultural values for sure, somehow we were still falling short.

After a very high-functioning finance director took some of this on, together we put more D&I initiatives in place. But companies can create an even safer environment for employees to discuss issues of harassment and unfairness, as well as providing clear lines of engagement when issues arise, when they hire a dedicated diversity and inclusion director.

According to the Society for Human Resource Management:

> The diversity manager develops, implements and monitors programs that promote diversity within the company. This role is responsible for developing training and initiatives to create and foster an open and inclusive environment. The diversity manager serves as the HR **ombudsman** for diversity issues.—Society for Human Resource Management

For companies with extremely lean overhead, I realize this can be a difficult head to justify. But a general business maxim I have subscribed to at each cycle is that "ownership equals results." As with all other business growth drivers (social media marketing, localization, customer support, etc.), nothing truly material happens at any company until it transitions out of being someone's part-time task. If you have someone whose full-time job it is to think about this by day and dream about it by night and they are also empowered, chances are you will see real change. Here's a list of how you can expect to see change with a diversity and inclusion officer onboard:

- Priority, visibility, and awareness of inclusion goals are sustained consistently, not ad hoc.
- More "boots on ground" to develop community outreach programs to bring greater diversity into your company. Someone can go to that WomenHack event, staff a booth, and attendees will see that you mean business.
- More horsepower to create different forms of diversity achievement goals in performance reviews throughout different functional areas. For instance, gender goals in engineering might be recruiting focused, while in marketing they are more about promotions.
- Ongoing education of you and your employees, including the use of diversity training programs and refreshers and new solutions occur.
- And, of course, clear goals are set with formal accountability. There is someone whose job it is to be accountable for this.

Words Can Change the World: Say "No" to Bad Behavior Regardless of Performance Level

Finally, I advocate that companies explicitly state in their employee handbook and company policy that making sexually suggestive comments to a coworker, if proven, is a fireable offense *regardless of performance*. Company handbooks routinely do this for more cut-and-dry offenses, such as if illegal substances are found at work, if illegal substances are being used, and if there is a physical altercation. These are all grounds for immediate dismissal, requiring little to no documentation or review process. So why does this not also exist for matters of discrimination and harassment where transgressions were clear and provable? Typically, the language that does exist at most companies focuses more on the victim's and witness's interpretation of "the existence of a hostile environment." Even less clear is the unhelpful suggestion for a remedy to "contact your HR representative." And in general sexual harassment cases are often treated more like a long-term performance correction than an illegal infraction. We tend to move much more slowly on them partly due primarily to internal team cultures and their tolerance for questionable behavior.

The time is now to take an explicit stance not to tolerate sexual harassment and prioritize the policy that it is a fireable infraction in employee handbooks and company guidelines. Having this explicit language is less about imposing a deterrent than it is about making it bonehead easy to decide quickly when problems eventually arise. While cases like Niniane Wang's are intrinsically more difficult because she and Justin Caldbeck did not work at the same company, cases like Megan Ferguson's need not be fraught with such ambiguity. Without a predetermined and explicit guiding policy, it was too easy for Megan's superiors to view high performance as the more influential factor to consider even despite many witnesses. Another benefit of explicit language is short circuiting the oftentimes consuming period of fretting and hand wringing experienced by victims of harassment. Do I report this or not? Will they *really do something?*

If you say: "Lewd and sexually suggestive comments are harassment; they will not be tolerated and constitute a fireable offense," you are saying, "I have your back." And in doing so, it is also highly helpful to have companion language to define specifically what sexual harassment looks like.

Recently, entrepreneur Cheryl Yeoh wrote a blog post, "Shedding Light on the Black Box of Inappropriateness," detailing her own experience with sexual harassment from 500 Startups Founder Dave McClure while raising funds for her startup accelerator. Cheryl had an epiphany; if the broad spectrum of sexual harassment was more crisply defined, it would make it much easier for a victim to report the incident to others without fearing the need to quote the perpetrator verbatim. The perpetrator either made a comment, directly propositioned by inviting, made a threat, or made a physical move. Her goal was to remove the common ambiguity surrounding transgressions, as well as to ease the burden for the victim. Yeoh's description for the four discrete levels of harassment paves the way for a standard industry-wide policy. This is also an idea Niniane Wang advocates. Here are Cheryl's definitions, excerpted with her permission:

LEVEL A. VERBAL OR GENDER HARASSMENT:

- Inappropriate comments, remarks, or suggestions that make the other party feel unsafe or uncomfortable
- Generalized sexist statements and behavior that convey insulting or degrading attitudes about women (e.g., insulting remarks, obscene jokes, and humor about sex or women in general)

LEVEL B. DIRECT SEXUAL PROPOSITIONS OR SEDUCTIVE BEHAVIOR:

- Unwanted, inappropriate, and offensive direct propositions or sexual advances (e.g., sexual invitations like "would you consider sleeping with me or coming to my hotel room?"; insistent requests for dinner, drinks, or dates; persistent messages, phone calls, and other invitations)

LEVEL C. SEXUAL BRIBERY OR COERCION:

- Solicitation of sexual activity or other sex-linked behavior with the promise of reward (e.g., funding, closing a deal); the proposition may be either overt or subtle
- Coercion of sexual activity or other sex-linked behavior by threat of punishment (e.g., negative performance evaluations, withholding of promotions, threat of termination)

LEVEL D. SEXUAL IMPOSITION:

- Unwanted and nonconsensual sexual imposition and physical advances (e.g., forceful touching, feeling, grabbing, kissing) or sexual assault

Cheryl further offers that companies can define their own A–D levels, or better yet, create an overarching standard policy for the entire industry. To me, her definitions are an excellent basis as is and would be value added for any of my companies to have as a working framework. If Megan Ferguson's HR department and her bosses had something like Cheryl's clearly stated harassment definitions, coupled with a decisive policy on which level of infraction would warrant punishment, then her situation would have turned out far differently. Both parties could have reacted much quicker.

But Wait, There's More

In addition to Cheryl Yeoh's harassment levels, I think there are some additional dimensions to consider. I recall a case where an incredibly talented male head of marketing at one of my companies, who was managing a mostly female marketing team, remarked off the cuff:

"If you think being a woman in tech is hard, try being a man in marketing!"

Source: iStock, Creatista.

At least one person in the room became uncomfortable with the comment. But when does this discomfort become harassment? While we took the employee's mention of her discomfort very seriously, in this case the comment did not seem sexual in nature. Gender referencing, yes. Sexual, not really. It was as though another set of parameters needed to be considered despite an employee's complaint. My HR director and I conferred and decided:

What should also matter:

- First acknowledge that some types of statements (like this one) are inherently more offensive to women than to men. In other words, acknowledge that this male employee's comment might have landed on female employee's ears differently than men's due to the inherent sensitivity of women to being usually the "out-group" in tech. That said, this comment equated being a man in marketing as being the same as the broader issue of gender discrimination against women, thus diminishing the significance of the latter.
- At the same time, not all offensive, profane, or even sexual language constitutes discrimination or harassment in the workplace.
- We then ask, was there intent to discriminate, to intimidate, or to belittle?
- Did the conduct persist unabated?
- Is there a pattern of similar insensitivity?
- What is the broader context in which the offensive conduct occurs?

In the end, we determined that while the remark was insensitive in that it was dismissive of some women's real struggles in industry, it was not sexual harassment and thus not close to being a fireable offense. I considered it a blessing that this incident occurred so we could test our own bracketing of what constitutes a fireable offense. I learned from this incident, and it gave us all an opportunity to reaffirm a company culture that supports everyone's ability to succeed and to do so in an evenhanded way.

In the end, what mattered most to all was that we paid attention. And as the Kapor Center advises on these matters:

Altering the company culture so that people were equally supported in their roles and given equal opportunities to succeed. This includes addressing discrimination and harassment in the workplace and penalizing people who are engaging in discrimination and harassment *no matter their level in the company.*

Laura Parmer Lohan
Founder, Ruckus Partners

Straight Talk: Do not order lunch.

"Do not ask a woman to take lunch orders. The next time you see a young female being asked to order lunch pull her aside and show her the link to DoorDash. And tell her to never take their order again. Want to know why men are so relaxed? Because men are just piling admin tasks on junior women's desk, and giving her no support. And on top of all of that, they are asking her to order their lunch."

7 | Solution 6: Adopt the ERA at Your Company—Because Your Country Didn't

Source: Jo Freeman.

Pierce City, Missouri, population 1,292, was founded in 1870 and named for Andrew Peirce Jr., president of the St. Louis–San Francisco Railway. When the United States Postal Service incorrectly spelled it Pierce, the new name stuck. After that inauspicious beginning, maybe the founders should have scrapped the whole idea of building a community as the town eventually became nationally known for a single horrific act.

In 1901, a white lynch mob killed three African American men who were accused of rape and murder. William Godley, French Godley, and Pete Hampton died by lynching. Pierce's white residents forced all remaining people of color out of town at gunpoint. Harrowing even for its day, that incident prompted Mark Twain to pen, "The United States of Lyncherdom," a biting essay denouncing both the intolerance and inequality of the nation.

The one bright spot to emerge from a town now stained with the lynchings was a woman named Martha Wright Griffiths. Born a decade after the racially motivated murders of the three young men by town folk, Griffiths would grow up and evolve into an important figure in the realm of women's rights. Raised by a father who believed that girls were innately smarter than boys and a mother determined to raise a young woman who could be economically self-sufficient, Griffiths realized both her parents' dreams. In 1934, she earned a bachelor's degree in political science from the University of Missouri and a law degree from the University of Michigan in 1940.

She practiced law alongside her husband, Hicks George Griffiths, until being elected to the Michigan House of Representatives in 1949. In 1954, she was elected to the U.S. House of Representatives. She became the first woman to serve on the powerful House Committee on Ways and Means. In 1982, she also became the first woman to be elected as lieutenant governor of Michigan.

According to *The Guardian*, "The weapons she deployed during her 10-term congressional career included implacable determination, a lawyer's grasp of procedural niceties, and a tongue like a blacksmith's rasp."

Source: U.S. Congress Archives (Michelle Strizevr)

The paper went on to call her "the mother of the Equal Rights Amendment," since she was the person who succeeded in bringing it closest to ratification.

The Equal Rights Amendment (ERA) is a proposed amendment to the United States Constitution designed to guarantee equal rights for all citizens regardless of gender. Ideally, it abolishes any legal distinctions between men and women in terms of property, employment, pay, divorce, and other matters. Every year that Griffiths served in the U.S. House of Representatives, she introduced ERA legislation. Keep in mind, when Griffiths started out in the House, there were 18 women (3.4%). Twenty years later, during her last term there were 16—an unfortunate decrease in representation for women.

Time and time again, Griffiths watched her bill die in the male-dominated Judiciary Committee. Finally, in 1971, amid the national clamor for racial and same-sex rights, the ERA finally passed both houses of Congress and was then submitted to the state legislatures for ratification in 1972. This victory occurred at the height of the women's movement and signaled to many the nation's readiness for change. Even so, getting the 38 states needed for ratification would be no easy task.

Revenge of the Housewife

Source: iStock.

By 1977, the amendment received ratification from 35 states. Congress gave the remaining states the deadline of March 22, 1979, to ratify the ERA. With significant support from both parties, including Presidents Gerald Ford and Jimmy Carter, it seemed like this would be victory for all women was in hand. But along came a "housewife" armed with an apron espousing traditional family values who asked fellow housewives to oppose the ERA. After a decade of Vietnam War protests, Watergate, and national racial and civil rights upheaval with long-haired, braless hippies featured as the agents of change on evening newscasts, the angry housewife's rally cry gained traction.

Phyllis Schlafly's "STOP ERA" campaign effectively halted the ERA's progress and doomed it to failure.

Phyllis Schlafly loved to position herself as a common housewife, opening her public speeches with her standard nod to being subservient in her marriage, "I'd like to thank my husband for letting me be here tonight." Despite the optics, Schlafly had nothing in common with the housewives of America. She graduated Phi Beta Kappa from Washington University in St. Louis, earned an MA in government from Radcliffe (sister school of Harvard) and a law degree from Washington University. Griffiths had been presented with a powerful nemesis of equal barrier-breaking status.

Schlafly's antifeminist movement, which began in 1972, used traditional symbols of the American housewife to gain opposition to the ERA. They took homemade bread, jams, and apple pies to state legislators with the slogans, "Preserve us from a congressional jam. Vote against the ERA sham" and "I am for Mom and apple pie." Interestingly, Schlafly's own childhood had been far from traditional. As a child during the Depression, Schlafly's father had lost his job and her mother worked multiple jobs and served as the primary breadwinner her entire childhood. Clearly, the reversed gender roles in the Schlafly household left the rising political activist with a firm sense that somehow her mother had been robbed of her rightful role.

"Many people who followed the struggle over the ERA believed—rightly in my view—that the Amendment would have been ratified by 1975 or 1976 had it not been for Phyllis Schlafly's early and effective effort to organize potential opponents," according to Jane J. Mansbridge in her book *Why We Lost the ERA*.

STOP ERA (STOP was an acronym for "Stop Taking Our Privileges") appealed to married women by fomenting fear. The group stoked fears by claiming that the amendment would repeal protective laws such as alimony and strip mothers of custody of their children in divorce cases. Antifeminists claimed that single-sex bathrooms would be eliminated and same-sex couples would be granted the right to marry if the amendment passed.

This strategy sounds eerily familiar, no? Women were told their daughters would no longer be exempt from the draft and passage would ensure that women would be forced to fight on the front lines alongside men. Wellesley College and other all-cherished female institutions would be forced to admit men!

Schlafly succeeded in positioning the ERA as a benefit only for "those other" young career women in cities. She warned that if men and women had to be treated equally, it would somehow threaten the security of middle-aged housewives with no practical job skills. In a matter months, a swelling tide of traditional stay-at-home women started to oppose the ERA.

In the end, the ERA was ratified in only 35 states, and of those, five states have tried to rescind their ratification. However, the Constitution doesn't allow for rescinding, so they remain on the record for ratification. Still, the pioneering perseverance of Rep. Martha Griffiths and the collective dream of reaching equality in the eyes of the law ultimately vaporized after decades of unrelenting effort.

Few people recognize that the ERA's most narrow defeat in 1976 was due not to inflexible entrenched men but rather ironically to a shrewd, empowered well-educated female leader. Once again this issue is more complex.

The Equal Rights Amendment was reintroduced in Congress on July 14, 1982, and has been unsuccessfully reintroduced before every session of Congress since that time.

Nowadays, longtime San Francisco activist Pam David believes there is a direct relationship between the failure to ratify the ERA and the woeful deficit of females in leadership positions.

Well, I do think some of it stems from not continuing to fight for the ERA. I mean, there is a piece that having civil rights does not solve. I mean, obviously it doesn't solve racism. It doesn't solve sexism either, but it's a line in the sand that lets you litigate, that brings consciousness to it. I feel like my generation, we stopped fighting in some ways for women's liberation. We got beaten down.

David, who is a lesbian, served in San Francisco government for over 12 years, working for three mayoral administrations and as a community organizer and activist on a range of civil rights and equity issues. Currently, she serves as executive director of the Walter and Elise Haas Fund, one of San Francisco's most-respected private foundations.

I mean if you look at the evolution in the great social movements in the 60s and 70s, so many of us were not just in one movement, we were in multiple movements and we brought that consciousness to it. There's also the lesbian/gay rights movement that came out of the women's movement which came out of the anti-racist movement.

It's not like we gave up, but we stopped fighting in the same way once the ERA did not happen and feminism became a target of ridicule on talk radio and we institutionalized some things. I was on the faculty at San Francisco State the first three years of a BA program in Women's Studies. But we somehow got isolated off and part of it is we were lefties. I mean a lot of us were, and not mainstream so we weren't trying to get into business, and there was too much to fight against whether it was Anita Bryant or Briggs Initiative and all of the reproductive rights struggles. We allowed the next generation of young women, we didn't fight with them about why it was important to identify as feminists. We kind of lost our edge in that we didn't pass it down in the same way. And so, now we have several generations of women who take their equality for granted, don't think they need to identify as feminists. Feminists got pigeonholed as bra-burners, as men haters, as marginal, we allowed it to be marginalized. At the same time we had made real openings, so people didn't feel the day-to-day exclusion of women that we did in our generation.

David was raised in suburban Highland Park, Illinois, which she describes as a "nice Jewish community" just outside Chicago. Along with her sister, who was one of the first women to attend law school, David's activism started early.

My very first political fight was fighting for the right to wear pants in high school, 1966. You know I mean that's ridiculous, right? But you forget there were so many visible manifestations of misogamy and sexism.

It was personal, you're telling me what I have to wear. Your prescribing to me that I need to do that? This is when the Vietnam War resistance had started, civil rights movement was in flow, and you're telling me that I can't be comfortable, that I have to, that you have the right to tell me what to wear.

It was a bunch of us. It was silly but it was meaningful and you often start organizing with issues that are personal. Then I did a lot of organizing against the war and organizing to lower the right to vote to 18 in Illinois. People we knew were being drafted without the right to vote, it was just wrong. There were a lot of us who got politicized in those years between 1964 and 1974.

David explains that part of the reason the ERA wasn't widely adopted by female activists had to do with the conservative nature of the National Organization for Women who "owned" the issue of passing the Equal Rights Amendment.

I came out when I was 22, 1974 to 75. I mean of that age our fights were with gay men for inclusion. Our fights were around infant mortality and bring a racial justice lens to reproductive rights.

There were a lot of other things going on. I think that a lot of us thought we were fighting sexism and misogyny and we'd made some advances and we were going to continue to do it. I don't think there was broad agreement that we needed any ERA.

I think it was a mistake, I think again it doesn't mean the fight is over, all of sudden there's no sexism, but I think giving up that fight had an impact. I think that is part of losing the next generations. If there had been a more grassroots and cross movement support to the ERA which also didn't happen. NOW was very isolated, NOW didn't work. They were racists. They were anti-lesbian. I don't think you build anything if you were siloed like that and narrow. There were so many things they would not talk about and they were purging people from their ranks. So I think if NOW had been a different kind of organization or if the cry for the ERA had been adopted by a broader set of folks it would have made a difference. I think NOW's ownership of the ERA narrowed the folks who cared about it, so when it died it just died.

Revive the Equal Rights Amendment: Ratify Now

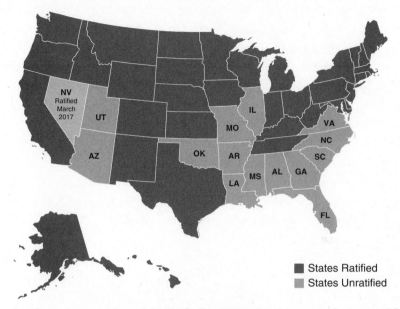

Against conventional belief, the ERA has not yet been ratified by the entire country.

Source: Equal Means Equal.

Even in today's divided nation, 96 percent of Americans believe women and men should be guaranteed equality in the Constitution. Additionally, nearly 72 percent mistakenly believe it already does. Taking a page from Pam David's early fight for the right to choose to wear pants in high school in the 1964, women and men need to embrace the fight for equal pay as deeply personal. Because equal pay for women is highly personal.

Employees, managers, and executive leaders should insist that the companies that employ them adopt the ERA in their corporate handbook. It's a human rights gap companies can easily fill. As chair of Geekwire, PicMonkey, and other companies and nonprofits, I believe in the notion of leading with one's values. Great employees want to be fulfilled not just by job content, but by the values their organization stand for. This is of course even more true with Millennials. Much more so than pay raises or free food, if you take a stand to demonstrate your values as a leader, you will attract passionate people and engender their loyalty long term. I believe in the power of concrete symbols and meaningfully crafted words, and know with conviction that if the ERA was widely adopted nationally and then companies mirrored its language, female employees I hire will know for certain that they are going to work in a safe place that values women. They won't wonder or have to dig through a long forgotten employee handbook to confirm whether we've opted in or not. And while the symbolic value is worth it alone, the actual relationship between legislation and workplace practices is also highly important. Proponents of the Equal Rights Amendment argue that what has been grossly missing is an overall guiding framework that clearly and unequivocally provides a legal foundation and a national standard that would radically alter the way companies handle women's rights. Without the ERA, the current state of affairs is akin to a smattering of discontinuous organs strewn about with no body. Equality for women has become an ideal that has been itemized, chopped into smaller digestible pieces with no overarching framework. It is a concept with no North Star.

Source: Stock photo.

Because of that, I think we are not one nation with shared values, united under the same ideals. I believe gender equality should not be handed out piece meal, state by state. With a broader women's movement at an all time high, the time is now for us to adopt the ERA across all 50 states and provide unequivocal protection against gender discrimination. With companies, industry, and the equality of women within industry in mind, let me offer three specific reasons why we need to pass the ERA (with inspiration and help from great organizations such as Equal Means Equal):

1. Companies follow the government's lead. Historically, it's only when the government clearly defines acceptable behavior through legislation, coupled with enforceable penalties for noncompliance, that companies take notice. Sadly, the stick is mightier than the carrot. Until such legislation is passed, companies should co-opt the ERA's wording as a matter of policy. For example in her book titled *Equal Means Equal*, Jessica Neuwirth writes that pregnancy discrimination is based on the presumption that "a worker is someone who does not become pregnant." Thus, equal rights legislation "would require recognition that women and men have biological differences and that the workplace cannot be structured solely around the biology of men."

   And again, many feel that the ERA would have prevented the case of Peggy Young, who was forced out of her job at UPS during her pregnancy because the company was not required to reassign her temporarily to a job that did not require heavy lifting. That's despite the fact that it was legally required to reassign workers with job-related injuries. The Supreme Court ruled 6–3 that "pregnant workers can claim the same accommodations that employers grant to large numbers of similarly restricted workers," according to *USA Today*. Imagine if this did not have to require a Supreme Court ruling!

2. Let's face it, it's embarrassing that the United States is behind other countries. For many reasons even beyond gender equality, perhaps now more than ever we need to raise the standing of the United States globally with respect to human rights and social justice. The elected officials and governing constitutions of many other industrialized countries in Europe and Asia have been affirming legal equality of women for decades. Why should we, the United States, be stuck in the nineteenth century?

3. Last, laws work best when they're crystal clear and explicit. And right now the Constitution is still woefully not clear. The closest constitutional wording to the concept of gender equality exists in the 14th Amendment's equal protection clause, dating back to 1868 postslavery Reconstruction times. It broadly asserts: "No state shall make or enforce any law which shall abridge the privileges or immunities of citizens of the United States; nor shall any state deprive any person of life, liberty, or property, without due process of law; nor deny to any person within its jurisdiction the equal protection of the laws." While the 14th Amendment has been applied to sex discrimination cases, the intent

was not to guarantee equal rights for women in the same way the Equal Rights Amendment would. In addition, while the 19th Amendment gave women the right to vote, late Supreme Court Justice Antonin Scalia insisted that the Constitution does not prohibit sex discrimination nor does it guarantee safeguard against gender discrimination. "Certainly the Constitution does not require discrimination on the basis of sex, the only issue is whether it prohibits it. It doesn't," he said in the January 2011 issue of *California Lawyer*. "Nobody ever voted for that."

As an imperfect document written by privileged men, the Constitution does not explicitly guarantee that all of the rights it protects are held equally by all citizens without regard to gender, and the only right that it specifically deems equal for women and men is the right to vote (19th Amendment, 1920). This has got to change.

All Is Not Lost

Before and after the defeat of the ERA, several discrete and narrower laws were passed that guarantee specific rights for women:

The Equal Pay Act of 1963 amended the Fair Labor Standards Act to explicitly state that no *employer* shall discriminate between employees on the basis of sex by paying a lower wage to one sex for an equal job.

Title VII of the Civil Rights Act of 1964 states in Section 703 (a) that it is unlawful for an employer to "fail or refuse to hire or to discharge any individual, or otherwise to discriminate against any individual with respect to his compensation, terms, conditions or privileges or employment, because of such individual's race, color, religion, sex, or national origin."

The Pregnancy Discrimination Act of 1978 amended the Civil Rights Act to "prohibit sex discrimination on the basis of pregnancy" or childbirth, and related medical conditions.

Title IX of the Education Amendment Act of 1979 stipulates, "No person in the United States shall, on the basis of sex, be excluded from participation in, be denied the benefits of, or be subjected to discrimination under any education program or activity receiving Federal financial assistance."

Pretty good, but we're not there yet. Even with these discrete advancements, women are still discriminated against in the workplace, lack leadership positions, and are paid less. According to a March 2017 *New York Times* editorial, the fact that the ERA never passed does have a lot to do with that, citing the United States rank at 45th in the 2016 Global Gender Gap Index (a ranking of countries according to size of gender gap from smallest to worse) below Europe, Trinidad, Namibia, and Laos. Predictably, the countries at the very top consistently have constitutional guarantees for women's equal rights. Interestingly, the editorial points out when the Nevada legislature recently endorsed the amendment in March of 2017, 35 years after the congressional deadline, it was a direct result of "the outrage of women and men at President Trump's sexism and vulgarity that resulted in millions of Americans marching in protest after his inauguration."

Perhaps Rep. Jackie Speier of California said it best when she told *USA Today* in a March 2017 interview: "If there ever was a time when it was right for us to finally get serious about passing the ERA, it's now." According to the *article*:

> The battle is more than symbolic, says Speier, with implications for how gender-based violence and workplace sex discrimination are addressed and litigated; for corporate standards involving accommodations for pregnant women; and for guaranteed access to prenatal care and contraception. It could also force a narrowing of the gender imbalance in top leadership roles. In countries with an equal rights amendment, women are represented in government in greater numbers. The U.S. ranks 104th, *behind* countries like Burundi, Serbia and Iraq.

Wow. 45th on the Global Gender Gap Index, and 104th in female representation in government. Let's get our act together. Let's ratify the ERA, for our country and our companies.

The Equal Rights Amendment:

Section 1. Women shall have equal rights in the United States and every place subject to its jurisdiction. Equality of rights under the law shall not be denied or abridged by the United States or by any State on account of sex.

Section 2. Congress and the several States shall have the power to enforce, by appropriate legislation, the provisions of this article.

Source: Stock photo.

Melody McCloskey, CEO StyleSeat

Straight Talk: Speak up.

"We will be at a meeting and you know someone will kind of raise their hand and say something really sweet. And I'm like I can't hear you. SPEAK LOUDER. You know that is a fantastic idea. You need to sell these ideas to me because if I don't hear them and you have that idea and it doesn't get to me, that's your fault. So part of being a good team member is speaking up, being present, being competent. Women need to be more direct."

8

Solution 7: Stand Together or Fall Apart

*"What I would like to say to all the women here today, is this: Women have been so oppressed for so long, they believe what men have to say about them. And they believe they have to back a man to get the job done. And there are some very good men worth backing, but not because they're men—because they're worthy. As women, we have to start appreciating our own worth and each other's worth. **Seek out strong women to befriend, to align yourself with, to learn from, to be inspired by, to collaborate with, to support, to be enlightened by.**"*
— Madonna's speech from 2016 Billboard Music Awards.

This is my most difficult chapter. There are times when as a man I wonder if I have permission to say the things I have already said in this book. When I speak specifically about what *men* can do to help women achieve equity, I don't feel like I need permission. But there is one last issue I need to address which pushes me into murkier waters. While I was doing research for this book, many women came forth to speak an uncomfortable truth: a common experience many women have had that adds friction to our path to gender equity. I was myself startled when it was first told to me, and it was only with the convicted and persuasive assurances of so many women that I finally admitted, yeah, this is a thing.

Is it the meat of the gender equality problem? No it is not. Maybe it's merely 10%. Maybe even less.

Should we overfocus on it? Most certainly not.

Does it absolve the current biased framework and its actors of responsibility? Heck no!

But is it real? Yeah, it is.

And what is the thing? It is that women do not always seize and take advantage of opportunities in the work place to support and cross leverage *each other* to the fullest extent.

For this reason, I have invited my colleague and friend Grace Kahng, who is assuredly much more eloquent than I am, to speak on this delicate matter. To me, Grace is the epitome of a strong, powerful female leader who has seen it all. A multiple Emmy Award–winning investigative journalist and documentary filmmaker dedicated to social justice issues, Grace has worked with the very best in the world because she herself is the very best. Most important, she has challenged me to think about sexism in a much more nuanced and complex way, from multiple angles. In keeping with the spirit of this book to sometimes speak the "uncomfortable truths" in order to lend truly meaningful discussion to the topic, I present to you Grace Kahng;

★ ★ ★

While Jonathan was proving himself as the wunderkind of Microsoft, successfully leading consumer and gaming teams, I was investigating mass-murdering Guatemalan officials, tracking pedophile priests, and winning hearts and minds at the Pentagon by exposing their role in illegally dumping military toxic waste.

In the same vein that Jonathan's life of being excluded initially shaped his fiercely inclusive leadership style, the engine that drove my interest in social justice and giving voice to the dispossessed was fueled by being told early and often that I was "less than," because I was born a girl into a traditional Korean family where the value of a daughter is defined by strict obedience and deference to men. This engendered a deeply felt loyalty to women which I carried with me from my earliest days of de-tasseling corn in the prairies of Minnesota to slinging deep dish pizza for tuition to working in network news for all the female broadcast "greats"—Diane, Connie, Oprah, Maria, Katie, and Meredith. I have watched often with acute pain the ways in which women do not seize and take advantage of opportunities in the workplace to support each other to the fullest extent.

Some of these behaviors are conscious, and some of them are unconscious. All of them have a sum negative impact on our ability as a group to gain equal footing with our male peers in the work place. In keeping with the notion that a rising tide lifts all boats, learning to recognize and correct our reaction or participation in bias in an intentional way helps all working professional women.

This chapter represents the smallest factor that mitigates female progress, but it is something 100% within our control. I do not think it makes me a bad feminist to bluntly call out negative reflexes. Nor do I believe that discussing our challenges with each other gives voice and ammunition to men seeking to justify their own backward behaviors and biases. I believe women have proven themselves smarter, stronger, and more flexible. We embrace critical feedback because we are naturally inclined toward self improvement. That is our magic. We can hear uncomfortable truths because we all survived middle school and we are tough. In interviewing hundreds of professional working women there were no shortage of anecdotes about the many ways in which women can sometimes unintentionally fail other women, and I think this warrants discussion. I have tried to identify a few behaviors for women to ruminate and remedy.

Touching the Third Rail

The toughest thing to hear when addressing a room full of empowered working women and discussing workplace gender equity is that sometimes, women don't support other women in the work place *enough*. It's like touching the metaphorical third rail on the subway. The person who raises the topic is going to get zapped. Some identify generational differences between competing groups of working women as an area of conflict. Others want to hold hands and sing "Kumbaya" and tell life-affirming stories of harmonious mentorship and success.

I'm "all in" for touching the third rail. Women *do* formally support each other and mentor each other in record numbers. Hurray! Research indicates that women who work in female-dominated environments experience greater job satisfaction. Mazel! But, data and a wealth of anecdotal interviews also indicates that the experience of *some* women working with other women in male-dominated environments like law firms and media and medicine can be less than ideal, *and here we can do something about it immediately, because it is 100% within our control.*

Female-to-female relationships in the workplace have improved and evolved significantly over the past 20 years. Linda Kozlowski, chief operating officer of Etsy, says it best:

> It is *more* common for women to support other women now. I definitely feel like there is a dramatic change in the way that I work with women colleagues now than when I did 15–20 years ago. Twenty years ago there was definitely a lot of jealousy . . . a lot territorial in nature, but now I feel like there is a much broader set of supportive women. At the same time: it is not perfect and unconscious bias does impact WOMEN as well. Women will often choose a male candidate unconsciously over a female candidate. **That to me is just as dangerous as men thinking that all the barriers are gone and women don't.**

Some women might think it verboten to discuss the notion of unsupportive behaviors and bias among women. While I appreciate and respect that viewpoint, some recent research attempting to quantify this shows that many women experience other women not being supportive at work. From a recent 2014 *Psychology Today* essay titled "Women Helping Women in the Workplace—or NOT?," researchers cited that a common form of what they call "in-group" competition:

> Indeed, a long-standing phenomenon in social psychology suggests "in-group favoritism" occurs such that people will show favoritism to members of their own social groups (Brewer, 1979, 2007). For a category such as gender, women should be evaluating other women more positively than they evaluate men.
>
> However, some studies have shown evidence contrary to these expectations such that in-group members do not show favoritism toward similar

others. There are even instances where people actually show a bias against their in-group members.

One reason that women might not support each other is to avoid a marginalized status in the workplace. Not providing support to other women might be a way to distance themselves from women as a marginalized group (Jackson et al., 1996). Rather than helping other women succeed, women might distance themselves from their female co-workers to avoid stigma and negative stereotypes.

More recently, research has shown that women may not support each other's progress specifically in situations where they are outnumbered by men. Ryan et al. (2012) found evidence that female supervisors were less supportive of female employees in male-dominated organizations.

The obvious question one might ask is: "But aren't there plenty of instances where men don't support each other in the workplace? Do women do this more than men?" From the research conducted by George Mason University's Psychology Department in 2012 titled "Exploring the Asymmetrical Effects of Gender Tokenism on Supervisor-Subordinate Relationships":

The results suggest that when women represent the minority in their working environment, they receive less support from female supervisors than do men or women working in a non-token [or non-minority] environment. The results support our expectations and demonstrate that the context of rare proportional gender representation influences female managers' support of subordinate women. The findings of this study illustrate that women who work in an environment where females are extremely underrepresented reported feeling *less* supported by female managers. Gender token status did not influence men's reports of support from male supervisors. According to these findings, one explanation for why women would be less likely to support same-gender subordinates resides in the context in which evaluations are made. The token women who doubly deviated from the male-dominated context were less likely to support same-gender subordinates, whereas the same was not true for men who are simply proportionally unrepresented.

"Double Deviation" means women are members of a group that is *both* proportionally scarce and of lower status, and it is because of this double deviation that women experience this friction from other women more so than men from each other given the same environment.

But I think perhaps yet another major factor this happens is that we women simply hold each other to higher standards than we hold men because we know we are smarter and more capable. We expect more of women. The bar is set higher. I'm not proud to say that I spent much of my career being extremely tough on my female employees. One of my early producers, Natalie Kossen Mashaal, reported, "Hands down you were my toughest boss but I love you for it. I owe you my attentiveness to detail." My longtime producer Erika concurred that I was the "toughest" boss she ever had (echoed by women and men in less glowing terms) but she had "learned the most." In retrospect I shudder at my unconscious reflexes. I tried to comfort myself by taking credit for Erika's success as the CEO of her own start up but Elliot, another employee, quipped, "It was either that or the grave." And while again it is NOT the main reason for the lack of women in leadership, it is real, and this is wholly under our own control.

Great Expectations: Case Study

By far and away the most difficult boss I ever had was a fierce woman. She was Dolores Umbridge without the syrupy sweet. While Marion Goldin shared Dolores's penchant for plaid Chanel jackets, Goldin was 100% jihad terrorist. Zero chance of backstabbing. She delivered body blows while looking you in the eye. When she trained her ire at you, you wanted to be on the other side of the world.

As one of the first females in network news, Goldin was the intrepid investigative *60 Minutes* producer for Mike Wallace. Her landmark investigations *made 60 Minutes* and set the standard for excellence in broadcast news magazine reporting for decades. And yet, unlike Morley or Mike or Ed, the public has no idea who she was despite her enormous contributions. The show was run by a man, and at the old boy network of CBS News, and the stories she told about men who tried to rattle her were memorable.

However, Marion was also the most unnecessarily sour human that I ever encountered professionally. Calling her tough would be an understatement. She was the first grown woman I ever witnessed telling men to "f*ck off" without batting an eyelash. I think "motherf*cker" was her favorite noun. She had countless stories about enduring Mike Wallace's mood swings and screaming editorial battles with Don Hewitt, the executive producer. I think it's fair to say that she really thought most men were fools. She was wickedly demanding but the best damn reporter/producer I ever worked for . . . right up until I quit in the middle of the atrium of a Disney hotel in Orlando after watching her pound her head against a glass table in anger over a perceived act of disloyalty. She was a terrible human being, but arguably the best damn producer in the business bar none.

There's no doubt in my mind that many of Goldin's appalling behaviors were shaped by being marginalized by male superiors on a daily basis. Had Goldin been born in a different era and surrounded by respectful female colleagues she would have been a completely different person. Broadcast news is and continues to be a male-dominated industry at the executive level. The recent revelations of bad behavior by Roger Ailes and Bill O'Reilly was not a fluke. I know countless reporters who as young women endured being grabbed, harassed, and groped.

The point is, there was no female bonding with Marion and a complete lack of personal interest. She intentionally kept her distance. There was no empathy, pleasant conversation, or discourse. The only three emotions I ever witnessed were impatience, anger, and extreme anger. Research like the ones cited above supports this notion that I have about Marion's lack of empathy for her female reports.

What is it specifically about female bosses in male-dominated work environments that creates a toxicity for women? Historians who study war point to insecure regimes as the most dangerous because they tend to lash out as a result of being deeply insecure about their survival. Executive coach, Shira Ronen, of Spectrum Consulting has seen all this and worked to help executives become better managers and leaders. Ronen says insecure managers are often at the vortex of a dysfunctional work environment.

When a boss is less secure they can't protect their people in front of others. There's always conflict. There's always blaming. When someone challenges the work, they are not going to say "No, my team actually did a really good job" and they are not going to be pounding the table and defending their team. They are also less likely to pound the table to request resources, help their team, and they are going to try to do everything themselves. When a boss is less secure, they are often not delegating enough, and they are trying to do too much and not giving enough opportunities for their team members. Often they aren't giving enough credit for their team because they are still trying to prove themselves. Unfortunately women tend to have this issue more than men, although I have worked with plenty of men who have had that phenomenon as well. Plenty.

Additionally, it is often much more difficult working for women versus men because the lack of support by a female manager might feel more "personal." Women are also socialized from an early age to be "liked," so when a work relationship doesn't translate into friendship it might feel like a personal failure.

We've seen what can sometimes happen when women are the minority in male-dominated environments, but what can also happen when females work or compete with each other in primarily *female-dominated* professions? While women might be sparse at the top, nursing is overwhelmingly dominated by women. Ninety-two percent of registered nurses in this country are women. One might expect that given this dominance, female nurses would naturally out of a sense of unity and sisterhood favor newly graduated female residents and offer female doctors an extra helping hand. "Not true," according to the early experiences of many female doctors, including Dr. Sabrina Thompson, who works at a large top-20 urban teaching hospital. Thompson says while she enjoys positive relationships with nurses in her current practice, as a resident she and her female residents felt bullied by many nurses. Perhaps this is similar to the unconscious biases of women that Linda Kozlowski referenced:

The thing about residency training is that the issue becomes more an issue clinically of working with the nurses. Historically the male residents are treated better by nursing staff. They cut them a little bit more slack. They tend to like them better. They tend to get along with them better. That don't give them as much sort of snitty pushback. And it's an unusual environment because it is the time that trainees are learning. They look to the nurses for a lot of their wisdom. And so there's this mixed power position. I think that the women get treated badly. And I was certainly treated poorly by nurses. And by female residents.

Sabrina says initially she was shocked by the sometimes inexplicable open disregard female nurses had for female doctors in training. Somehow the experience felt oddly competitive instead of collegial.

> We were on call overtime all the time. When we get called for you know to see a patient in the middle of the night. The male resident comes in and the nurses pat him on the back, but if I mention I was exhausted, do you know what did they say to me? "Well I didn't choose this job, you chose this role, that's why you're here." That type of sassy things sort of cut people down, and make you feel weaker and more exhausted. You're already at your low; they kick you in the shins.

As someone who surrounds herself with strong female friendships, Sabrina says the irrationally negative treatment she and other female physicians receive from their fellow female support staff can be acutely crushing.

On the other hand, Genentech's Dr. Ellie Guardino, former head of Stanford's Cancer Research Lab, says she has only enjoyed *positive* supportive relationships with female nurses. She offers some possible insight into Thompson's experience and female-to-female friction. Guardino spent decades at Stanford treating women with late stage breast cancer. She says there might be something else at play when it comes to women working with other women peers.

> I think there may have been nurses that held me to a higher standard than male colleagues but that might because they knew I was smarter! Women know that women are smarter than the men so they just feel sorry for the men and so they feel they have to support them more.
>
> When I think about my relationship with my daughter, I think I have a higher standard for my daughter then my sons. I actually notice that because I relate so well to or have certain assumptions about my daughter and the way her brain works. I wonder if the bias is in holding other women to a higher standard.

It's Really Not Personal

In a recent 2016 study released by Professor Sun Young Lee of UC School of Management titled *"Competitive Workplaces Hold Women Back,"* she concluded that one of the biggest barriers to female career advancement is: other same-gender colleagues. Lee's paper concludes that women are more likely to fall out with female colleagues whom they suspect of trying to elbow them aside on the career ladder than they would with men. Similar to the George Mason University research, when women are the underrepresented group at work, they may see fewer opportunities for personal advancement. This drives the need to treat other women more negatively to eliminate threats to advancement.

But there is a systemic cause here. Professor Lee said the findings suggest that standard career structures in which people are constantly encouraged to compete for promotion ("kill and win") put women in particular at a disadvantage. Lee's study argues that this is because while men view competition and hierarchy as a natural and accepted part of life, so-called female peer culture is effectively the opposite—valuing harmony and the appearance of equality. As a result, women could be damaging their own career prospects by overreacting to competitive behavior in the office, taking competition too personally. She argued that bosses need to be acutely aware that competitive career structures that are effective to men may be detrimental to women, and also that on the flip side, *women should learn that taking competition from other women too personally could be holding them back in leadership positions.*

That's music to Debbie Landa's ears. A veteran female entrepreneur in tech and COO at StyleSeat, Landa also points out that junior women often have a tough time taking feedback from women versus male superiors. She wants women to consider the current business playing field and understand that competing is "not personal" or a bad thing.

As a man you get rewarded for not only winning but crushing your opponent. It's conditioning. Men play on sports teams, right? And if they don't play on a sports team they play computer games. As a man you are trained to kill and win, right? You go for it and that is how these boys are brought up. Other men validate your feeling of crushing and winning and that you are a MAN, that is the validation: the more you win the more you're a man. And for women that would be horribly aggressive to even show that you salivate for winning. It is so unbecoming of a woman. Afterwards, all the men walk off the field and get a beer. No hard feelings. That's not true for women.

Come Together: Right Now!

Sexual harassment whistleblower Niniane Wang suggested that the inability of women to come together as a cohesive supportive political group in the same way that minorities have coalesced as a movement, thwarts meaningful progress as does the lack of one leader.

> Before Martin Luther King, there probably was a lot of infighting. Just like in companies, when there is no CEO, all the VPs are fighting against each other. I think there's leadership missing. Like a Gloria Steinem. I think of the cause of gender rights in Silicon Valley as similar to a work situation. If we were a company, there'd be issues because there is so much infighting and not enough clearly articulated goals. Everybody wants different things and some people are very outraged and it's just very disorganized.

Wang says by far and away the most distressing part of going public with the Caldbeck story was watching women continue to support Binary Capital cofounder Jonathan Teo. Wang feels strongly that Teo knew about his partner's predatory behavior and did nothing to stop him. In her mind, Teo's lack of action was more damaging because had he acted to stop Caldbeck, fewer women would have been abused and humiliated.

> I think that the most disheartening thing that I experienced was when women spoke out against me. I mean they weren't literally against me but they were against the things I wanted. Like this one story—this woman texted me "You're a hero!" when I spoke out against this predator. But then five days later, people started texting me to look at her Facebook and I'm looking and she had written this great, long post about his enabler, Jonathan Teo, and how Jonathan Teo is so amazing, we all need to support him. And I knew Jonathan Teo was aware of Justin's bad behavior and was enabling.
>
> And I pointed this woman to Teo's initial statement about how there was nothing improper and the allegations were false. And there was a long pause and she was trying to struggle with what to do. And then she asked if I could compromise. And I said I would not compromise on defending women and, you know, I stopped talking to this woman. But I think that was very, very disheartening because it does feel like you are sacrificing your own time and reputation to help other women. And then when you see other women come out against you—the people you were trying to

help—it just feels very pointless. Like you have made this sacrifice for them and then they are angry at you. It feels very disheartening.

The power of women united in voice and outrage is evidenced by the impact that Niniane Wang and the other victims of Justin Caldbeck has had on the issue of sexual harassment in Silicon Valley. In 2012, Ellen Pao's allegations of abuse against her powerful Kleiner Perkin's partner failed to ignite meaningful support and outrage among women in technology. Five years later professional women in Silicon Valley are unwilling to give blatant sexual bullying a pass. Within weeks of the report about Justin Caldbeck an avalanche of other women came forward with their own hideous stories of unwanted sexual overtures which resulted in the resignation of some of the most popular and influential venture capitalists in Bay Area tech. To Niniane's point, there is powerful magic when women work together to foment change and attack challenges of inequity as a group rather than allowing powerful men to pick off women one by one.

Our Unique Strengths as Women

I love women. I believe women are far more capable then men in every facet of life. Despite the early challenges of being born female, given the choice, I would never come back as a man. Being a woman means we are more complex and it is a tremendous gift. Just look at the biological evidence. That extra chromosome is not insignificant. We might not be as good at putting ourselves forward or negotiating as long and hard or advocating for ourselves but women have proven time and time again to be unparalleled problem solvers and visionaries. A great example of this is the aforementioned Dr. Ellie Guardino, whose life and work underscores the very best of what a woman can do and contribute.

At 52, oncologist and mother of three, Dr. Ellie Guardino is in the final stages of battling metastatic melanoma. As the Vice President of Product Development at Genentech and a Stanford oncologist who dedicated her career to shepherding women and their families through late-stage breast cancer; she refuses to quit advocating for life. Her technical expiration date was February 2017, and yet on March 29, Ellie traveled to Washington, DC, with IV in tow (administering herself chemo in her hotel room) and presented in front of the FDA and won approval for a revolutionary new cancer treatment drug her team developed called Rituxan.

As her friend and longtime Stanford Cancer nurse Chris Tucker describes, "She's young, compassionate, and beyond brilliant. Her ability and her drive to get things done are unparalleled. You would think somebody like that, that you would meet some rough old battle axe who has spent her whole life pushing people around to get her way. But she's not. She works her butt off for the sake of her patients, but she exudes warmth and she's personable and you just want her to be your best friend."

At a recent prayer vigil and appreciation for Ellie, hundreds of friends and former patients showed up to celebrate her life's work and dedication to patients and their families. One by one, former patients or their survivors spoke eloquently about her impact on their lives and the grace with which she helped loved ones prepare for their final days. Ellie is uniquely female and she argues that is specifically what makes her and other women better physicians.

> Women have a much better EQ. So, not only do I think that women are pretty smart but they have more EQ. My friend, a male nurse, was saying last week about how male-dominated medical world is so unfortunate because the female doctors really provide a more holistic care for the patient. In his experience female physicians are better at addressing things that are more critical and spending more time with the patient.
>
> In oncology it is critical that you have the holistic approach to the patient. You're not just taking care of the patient, you are taking care of the family. You are taking care not just the medical care—more about the cancer journey and the support they need. When I walk in with a new patient there are so many questions that I need to ask. What is your social support? What are your worries? How are you going to get to appointments. Who is there to help you?

It was this holistic approach that revolutionized the Stanford practice's approach to fertility for women diagnosed with late stage breast cancer.

> My male colleagues had not addressed the fertility issues for patients and we completely changed the way we care for breast cancer patients and ensuring that they have options.
>
> Instead of saying, "Well, we are curing you and so you shouldn't be worried about the fertility issues; its more important to be alive," it should be "Let's keep you alive and not compromise your options at the same time."

Guardino is revered by patients battling cancer who have survived and now have children because Stanford hired their first female faculty for the breast cancer program.

To me, Dr. Ellie Guardino is the prime case study of the how women uniquely contribute to solving problems and creating value in the work-place and for the greater good. Nurses love Ellie. The female doctors and researchers at Stanford and her Genentech team sing her praises. But sadly, not all female supervisors share Ellie's brand of supportive mentoring. We need more Ellies versus Marions.

There are signs of hope and progress at every turn. I will leave you with this inspiring development. In May 2017, for the first time in its 125-year history, the Sierra Club elected an all-female executive committee to oversee its 3 million members and supporters. Board President Loren Blackford and her executive committee have very intentionally taken turns speaking out publicly about Sierra Club's objectives. "Step up and step back is more my leadership style. I think it is my job to elevate as many diverse voices as possible. I believe in leading from behind. To really increase your power and your reach, you need to have as many people possible leading in the best way they can toward your shared aims."

Wow. Kudos to Blackford for her refreshingly female-forward style of leadership. Through actions big and small women can address and over-come their own unconscious biases and work to stand together to move the football down the field. How long, I wonder, will it take to get 100 female CEOs to lead the Fortune 500?

Debbie Landa
CEO, Deal Maker Media

Straight Talk: Don't always follow the rules.

"Women have so much internal pressure to follow the rules. They forget that this is a game and we are in it to win it. Sometimes you have to color outside the lines. Men do it all the time and they don't have to get along with everyone. They just want to be respected. Women have to be reminded we are here to f*cking win and we are going to win at all costs."

Shelley Ross
Former Executive Producer of Good Morning America, ABC News; Former Executive Producer of CBS This Morning

Straight Talk: "There is a double standard between the way men and women are evaluated with leadership. The bar is so much higher for female executives. The one thing I heard often was I wasn't nurturing enough. I wasn't a nurturing personality. No one expects that of men. No one would criticize male executives for not being nurturing enough. By the way, I mentored plenty of women who to this day write me the nicest emails and I'm proud of these relationships which endure."

9

Solution 8: The Future: Raising Better Men

I'm glad we've begun to raise our daughters more like our sons, but it will never work until we raise our sons more like our daughters.

—Gloria Steinem

Not having a father early on, I've spent much of my life thinking about conventional notions of manhood and what it means to fit into that. I would imagine that all men think about this at some stage in their lives. For me it started young when I didn't feel comfortable joining other boys in the teasing of a socially awkward or unpopular classmate. When I returned to the United States at the age of 9 from living abroad in Hong Kong, the ire of the masses briefly turned on me when the bigger, "cooler" American kids teased me for my hair, my clothes, or just simply being Asian. Those tough times galvanized me into someone who figured out how to stand his ground—to learn that "might is right" on the playground (at least back in the 1970s); and when you smack a bully in the jaw, they stop bothering you.

I also learned that boys and girls were supposed to hate one another. "Girls germs no returns!" was a constant refrain among my new elementary school friends. "Throwing like a girl" was a new type of insult, unfamiliar to me as there was no equivalent phrase in Hong Kong. I liked playing with the girls at recess on occasion. They adopted me into their circle, and I never once heard a racist slur hurled at me from any of them. I liked being around their noncombative play style, until I was made to feel wrong for being there.

As my body grew tall and strong, eventually I learned that the formula for high school popularity was to simply play the right sports, drive a cool car, and not make too many mistakes with girls, and I would grow to be a popular scholar athlete who became a homecoming prince and student body president. The same year that my football team was going to state, I recall running off the field from finishing practice, pads, cleats, helmet and all, right into a waiting chess club match. I joined the chess club just that year as a sort of last-minute act of subversion to celebrate geek power. Those early tough times being picked on in elementary school taught me the pain of being an "outsider" and "less than." I appreciated the journey that I had endured and wanted others to know that they, too, can rise up. It's all in how you work the system; it's just a game that you play.

In college, I pledged a fraternity. Instant friends. They seemed like good guys, but I was encouraged to hate the guys next door and fight the ones across the street, who seemed pretty much just like us but with their hair parted on the *other* side. They were to be competed against . . . who had the best party . . . who drank the most . . . who got the most girls . . . who raged the hardest.

The pretty sorority women were sort of conquests. I had an amazing date with one of most popular upperclassman women...a coming of age moment worthy of John Hughes and Wilt Stillman...only to have it cheapened by the prying and incessant questions of other guys who wanted to know every private detail...women were not our partners, they were game, "the other side." Enough of my female friends shared stories of misbehavior that I cofounded a group on campus called SASA, or Students Against Sexual Assault. With the full cooperation of the college, the educational programs we devised gave us a poignant and clear window into the harsh realities many young women face the moment they step foot onto a college campus.

Upon graduating and coming of age in the early 1990s, young men were often given mixed messages—imagery of male heroes in popular culture were still either Rambo or Richard Gere from *Pretty Woman*—you should either be muscular or rich. And before you knew it, you entered the workforce in earnest and found yourself amid "brogrammers" and alpha geeks.

Now with an 8-year-old boy of my own, I want to feel like we live in much more evolved times. I feel like we're almost there, but not quite. My son's classroom in an in-city Seattle neighborhood is 50 percent nonwhite, many of whom are of mixed heritage. When I ask my son to describe a new friend, he does not lead with, "He is African American...." but, rather, "He loves Minecraft as much as me!" Boys and girls routinely play together with no hesitation. Never once have I heard "girls germs no returns!" on his playground. When I ask him who at his school is best in sports or math, the answers are Nora, Leah, and Beckett. Requests are frequent and common for cross-gender playdates. When girls and boys play together, they do so collaboratively and with equal sharing of roles heroic or needing adventurous assist. When I asked my son who his best friend was, he said, "Nora." And encouragingly, new science validates that we're on the right path. A recent Arizona State University study found that children who are encouraged to play with friends of the opposite sex developed much better problem solving and communication.

And while I know that as my son grows this might change, I also know that my wife and I have a shot at laying a better foundation. Like young bones and muscles that become stronger when training begins early, gender attitudes can be similarly strengthened at a young age. It is precisely this time when we have a shot at raising a better generation of men. To the best of my ability, we have tried to do the following.

Show That Mom Is Incredible and Strong

Dads, for many of us it goes without saying that we should all break from what we grew up with and get our domestic game on. This is really many things that include not splitting housework along traditional gender lines, as well as division of decision making. If the boy sees only mom cooking and doing laundry while dad chops wood and tunes the car, narrower gender definitions become calcified in the child's mind. And there is much we can do daily to reinforce that:

- Mom is equal. Kids overhear a lot and understand much. I was struck by one conversation with my son where he picked up on that I somehow was often the one with final signoff on major purchase decisions. This diminished the sense of equality between us in my son's eyes and caused me to make sure that I consulted my wife on major financial decisions for her approval from that point forward. Yes, I admit that I made a bit of a show of it at first in front of my son, but it was important to demonstrate this overtly.

- Mom can have a career, too (if she wants). This can actually benefit your children down the line. In an article from Oxford University Press's *Quarterly Journal of Economics* titled "Mothers and Sons: Preference Formation and Female Labor Force Dynamics,"[1] a growing presence of a new type of man is cited. The article presents evidence, accumulated over the years, that shows a powerful correlation between mothers who work and their sons; wives of men whose mothers worked are themselves significantly more likely to work and be supported in their careers. It also found that sons of women who work for any amount of time before age 14 spend more time on housework and child care as adults.[2] This is what I call a high-leverage situation that we harness for continual improvement for future generations. So let's also foster mom's career, for both its immediate benefits and for its value for future generations.

Communicate Differently at Home

What if we applied the knowledge from "Listen Louder" to practice at home? What if cross-gender-style verbal communication was not just limited to the men raised by single mothers? We know that men and women have different speaking styles. If we continue to maintain the male style as the norm even at home, we are then committing to continue penalizing women. If men put to practice the concepts of active and empathetic listening, cooperative dialogue, catching bids and "turning toward" in the home sphere, sons and daughters would have adequate modeling for the future, and we might begin to reset the norm.

In *Man Made Language*, Australian feminist scholar Dale Spender speaks of how in patriarchal societies men control language to sustain norms in their favor regardless of context: "Language helps form the limits of our reality. It is our means of ordering, classifying and manipulating the world."[3]

And if men are responsible for an unfair system where men are the norm and women are "less than," then Spender, like me, objects to women having to do all the changing. If men currently own the right of way, men must also own its dismantling. As I've argued, women shouldn't be doing all the changing. Let's teach our sons how to speak with inclusion and empathetically so that they in turn value it when others do the same. Again, men must be the change. Let's show our sons how to be great listeners at home as well as the office.

Break Out of the Man Box and Call Out Bro Behavior

We need to teach our boys to speak up when others are wrong. When VC Justin Caldbeck was cited for bad behavior by Niniane Wang, much was discovered about others around him who were willing to look the other way. And while I value loyalty and friendship as much as most, we need to teach our boys to understand the threshold past in which the greater good is compromised. This is a difficult problem that begins with young men's inherent longing to "stay in the box." In a landmark 2017 international study called "The Man Box," researchers Brian Heilman, Gary Barker, and Alexander Harrison define the Man Box as a set of beliefs that place pressure on men to conform to a standard and behave in a certain way while protecting normative male behaviors.[4] Generalized across several cultures (United States, United Kingdom, and Mexico) by a study of 1,000 young men between the ages of 18 and 30, these beliefs are things like self-sufficiency, acting tough, sexual aggressiveness, physical prowess, and the use of physical force as a way to resolve conflict. What is accepted behavior for young men is collectively defined by those in the box. To be a man is to *always* remain in this box. Going outside the box is stressful and reviled. Protect the box at all costs.

But more tellingly, life in the Man Box can often breed "negative repercussions for young men themselves, for young women, and for others in their lives. . . . In the United States and U.K., men in the Man Box are *six times more likely to report perpetrating sexual harassment.*"

In fact, three of the seven pillars of the Man Box are about aggression and control, sexual dominance, and factors accretive to aggression towards women.

But there is hope. Not every young man needs to be trapped inside. There are those emergent young men observed in the study who are "outside the Man Box," and have broken out to embrace more positive, equitable ideas and attitudes about how "real men" should behave, demonstrating that it is possible to reject these rigid ideas about manhood. They openly decry sexism. They speak out against inequality. They call bullsh★t on harassment. But it is not easy for them. These same young men are much more likely to report exclusion, self doubt, and social isolation. Thus, Heilman, Barker, and Harrison call on all of us:

> All of us, as young men and young women, parents, educators, the media, teachers, romantic partners, and members of society, need to be part of the process of reinforcing positive, equitable, unrestrictive ideas of manhood— in other words, of breaking the Man Box. It is time for all of us to work to break this destructive cycle and to break the Man Box.

And in the same way that I support more research on non traditional leadership styles, I would love to see more research on practical strategies for how we cultivate and support more "out of Man Box" culture in our society.

Show Him That Things That Are Traditionally "Feminine" Are Not "Less Than," or Off-Limits

When my son was 5, he became entranced with a particular box in the garage of our house. It was not a box of my old robot action figures nor old comic books. It was a box from my wife's own childhood, containing a vast array of Barbies, troll dolls, and at least one Donny and Marie Osmond pair. As my wife gingerly laid out the very pink contents of the box on the living room floor, we were acutely aware of our own unspoken biases and apprehensions. But she also committed to the notion that he should never be told that there is anything wrong or "less than" about any of his mother's old toys. She wanted him to normalize to many of the accoutrements of 1970s' girl play, to pretend bake with the toy oven, to style Mr. Troll's hair, and (my personal favorite), to make Donnie Osmond wear a decidedly more fierce outfit. In doing so, we intended to show him that "girl activities" were never off-limits or, worse, "less than" for a boy.

As it turns out, mixing it up is a good idea. In fact, don't even begin to ascribe gender to toys at all. Washington and Lee University professor of psychology Megan Fulcher says,

"Play with masculine toys is associated with large motor development and spatial skills and play with feminine toys is associated with fine motor development, language development and social skills. Children may then extend this perspective from toys and clothes into future roles, occupations, and characteristics."

It would seem that in addition to intrinsic language differences that begin to bifurcate girls and boys in early development as cited earlier by Carol Gilligan, we may be further segregating girls and boys into gender stereotypical job occupations by simply making toys gender specific. In 2008, Fulcher's research also found that children with gender-stereotyped decorations in their bedrooms held more stereotypical attitudes towards boys and girls. Let's put an end to gender barriers in play. Let him play with "girl toys." And also let sis play with "boy" ones.[5]

Show Him New Heroes, Stories That Include Women and Girls

I believe it is time our sons start reading and seeing more media with female and non white heroes. We need a preponderance of films, books, and especially video games that pass the Bechdel-Wallace test, where female characters carry forth the narrative without the need for men or talking about men. Let's show our sons that women are just as capable as leaders, heads of states, CEOs, and superheroes.

And I can offer a great economic argument. In one of the most encouraging studies in recent years commissioned by a talent agency, CAA, it was found that there is a much stronger correlation than previously believed between diverse casting and box office success at the highest levels. As recently as 2016, the Oscars and by extension all of Hollywood was considered laggards on gender equality and diversity. For decades films with women and blacks as leads were considered "risky" and not worthy of higher-tier budgets. But this highly data-driven CAA study showed that in fact, at every budget level, a film with a cast that is at least 30 percent nonwhite—that was CAA's definition of a "truly diverse" film—outperforms a release that is not diverse in opening weekend box office. And as a matter of fact, the very best-performing movie of the films evaluated, which had an approximately 40 percent diverse cast and a 38 percent diverse audience, was *Star Wars: The Force Awakens*, starring a strong female Daisy Ridley as the central protagonist. And on track to be one of the highest-grossing films of 2017, *Wonder Woman* has already broken several records including best second weekend box office of any modern superhero movie. A female lead is now the leading box office superhero movie. Let's make more.

We have before us a captive audience in the current generation of boys. For the first time, parents of girls and boys are more engaged than ever. We care deeply that the world becomes better for them than it was for us. Women's issues are not just front and center in media but civic demonstrations and public marches are at historic highs. If we take this opportunity to show that women are incredible, that they are to be valued as equals not conquered, we may have a shot. If we teach our boys to break out of the box, listen better to women, and create more expansive definitions of leadership that recognize women's unique qualities, then we may have a shot. If we never use the phrase "you throw like a girl" as an insult, but instead as a compliment, then we may have a shot. And finally, if we celebrate women's long-deserved status of being capable badass Jedis and world saving superheroes, then yes indeed, I become hopeful that we have a fantastic shot at the next generation being truly "better together."

Grace Kahng
CEO, Santoki Productions

Straight Talk: "I believe it to be true that you find your family at work. Whatever dynamics you experienced growing up, you will bring into the work place so it behooves everyone in the work place, particularly women, to have done their psychological work so that nobody else is able to take advantage of them in ways they aren't aware of. Often women learn to diminish themselves if they grow up in a family where they were diminished and so it's hard to step out beyond one's comfort zone if they didn't do it in the family."

10 | Final Thoughts

I believe we are at the cusp of change. With the cascading resignations of so many men who have been called out for sexist behavior, and the public celebration of companies and individuals who support women's advancement, perhaps for the first time a dam has truly broke and more sweeping change will continue to occur. While many may lament that public discourse of equality are only temporary, testing only the elasticity of the current framework but ultimately leaving it intact, I believe otherwise. I believe all revolutions require three things: time, heroes, and momentum. All great revolutions take time. The undercurrent of the French Revolution spanned a century when taking into account the preceding years of enlightenment. The American Revolution, a period often depicted in schoolbooks to seem like a quick and violent guerilla war, itself spanned nearly 20 years. The civil rights movement was a decade in itself and arguably still evolving. So leading with women shall too take its time, and I am hopeful we are near the end, with years of preceding discourse and "enlightenment" not in vain.

And this too shall require heroes. We have Ellen Pao, Niniane Wang, Sallie Yoo, Erika Trautman, Pam David, Charlotte Guyman, Cheryl Yeoh, and many, many others. And I believe there will be more who will not stand for the status quo and also come forth and activate others. As my hero Niniane Wang offered me:

We have to continue working at this . . . setting goals like it's work . . . accomplishing goals one by one. There's a lot of preparation that goes into it: amassing evidence, establishing a pattern, taking a clearly articulated goal, building support towards that goal, etc. At first I thought my goal was to simply get the story out there.

So that was my only hope. Then once he took a leave of absence, I realized, wow, I actually could help make that permanent so that it really protects women. But then I spent all weekend working towards that goal and figuring out what actions would help convince people to make his leave of absence permanent. And then once that had happened, there was his enabler. And I knew that his enabler had truly enabled him. So I didn't want that person to be in a position of power anymore. And I felt . . . people who enable and turn a blind eye to years of harassment should not also be in positions of power . . . So then I turned my eye towards that goal and was acting towards that goal . . . Next week, I want whatever the thing is next week. And then the following week. And then next month. And then gradually over five years . . . yeah we're going to gradually get there.

And when I asked Niniane what she would now tell all men?

Now I'd like men to truly listen . . . Truly listening for hours to women and their stories and being able to put themselves in the shoes of the women. I think sometimes people think, oh, equality means I should be blind to gender. I should treat every woman the same as I treat a man. I should never ask her about gender. I think that that's also not the best way. Because then you won't understand the unique challenges and what the problems are. So if men just spent five hours just talking to women entrepreneurs and understanding the struggles that they face, then they will be able to do the right thing for their situation to help.

Thank you, Niniane. I couldn't agree more. And for those men who have already come forth to help, bravo. And for those on the sidelines, may you finally join us men and women in being the change. Let's make the world better for our daughters and sons. Let's finally crest this hill.

A Note from Niniane Wang

In June 2017, two decades into my career as a technology leader and executive, I went on the record with five other women to expose sexual harassment by venture capitalist Justin Caldbeck. After an intense period of making rebuttals to his firm's press releases and requesting accountability from the firm's investors, our actions led to Justin's resignation. This kicked off a string of sexual harassment revelations over the next weeks. So far, we've seen resignations of six CEOs and venture capitalists and the closure of a $175 million venture fund.

Many people asked how I decided to be the first person to go on the record. Part of it was the desire to do the right thing. Another part was because I knew what "normal" should look like. I know how it feels to be respected by colleagues and feel safe in a professional environment. This is due to years of working with men like Jonathan Sposato.

I first worked with Jonathan at Microsoft Games when I was 19 years old in my first full-time job. I remember his humorous emails to groups of coworkers, describing his mother's antics such as her admonitions about feng shui. Jonathan did not believe in feng shui, but he took his mother's feelings seriously. I saw that Jonathan was a gentleman, and it created a positive example in my young mind.

Eight years later, I was working day-to-day with Jonathan at Google after his first company was acquired. We were leaders for a product I had chartered, Google Lively. I admired Jonathan's high emotional intelligence quotient. During one critical period of the project, the urgency level was high, and one meeting grew heated. Jonathan expertly calmed down the room and set us back on a productive track.

I visited Jonathan in Seattle a few times. Once, I went with him as he swung by the restaurant he owned, the Spitfire. While there, a female employee walked up to him nervously and explained a predicament they were facing. Jonathan made a quick decision to unblock her situation. As she turned to walk away, he stopped her to commend her for doing a good job. The anxiety on her face morphed into relief and pride.

Jonathan is calm and respectful whether he is speaking with his wife, a work colleague, or the CEO of Google. It is only with allies that we can collectively make enough progress to achieve gender equality. I'm thankful that I've had Jonathan as an ally for 20 years.

The long-term fix for reducing harassment is to achieve a 50-50 gender split in the workplace, because hypermasculine environments are the breeding ground of harassment. Jonathan has written this book to help us work toward that long-term goal.

Niniane Wang
CEO of Evertoon

Endnotes

Not Enough Women? Look Harder

1. Jeffrey Joseph, What Companies Use Blind/Anonymous Resumes and What Benefits Have They Reported? Ithaca, NY: Cornell University ILR School. Available at http://digitalcommons.ilr.cornell.edu/cgi/viewcontent.cgi?article=1108&context=student.
2. Jeff Barrett, "If You Care About Resume Gaps, You're Missing Out on This Valuable Demographic," *Inc.*, June 19, 2017. Available at https://www.inc.com/jeff-barrett/3-million-experienced-women-are-ready-to-jump-back-into-the-workforce-and-some-.html.
3. Isabel Metz, Anne-Wil Harzing, and Michael J. Zyphur, "Of Journal Editors and Editorial Boards: Who Are the Trailblazers in Increasing Editorial Board Gender Equality?" *British Journal of Management*, September 10, 2015.

Listen Differently

1. Carol Gilligan, *In a Different Voice: Psychological Theory and Women's Development* (Cambridge, MA: Harvard University Press, 2016).
2. Tara Sophia Mohr, *Playing Big: Find Your Voice, Your Mission, Your Message* (New York: Penguin Random House, 2015), p. 181.
3. Erika Trautman, interview by Grace Kahng, July 15, 2017, transcript.
4. Alison Wood Brooks, Laura Huang, Sarah Wood Kearney, and Fiona E. Murray, "Investors Prefer Entrepreneurial Ventures Pitched by Attractive Men," *Proceedings of the National Academy of Science of the United States of America* 111, no. 12 (2014): 4427–4431. www.pnas.org/content/111/12/4427.full.

5. Maha Ibrahim, interview by Grace Kahng, June 22, 2017, transcript.

6. Joseph Folkman and Jack Zenger, "What Great Listeners Actually Do," *Harvard Business Review,* July 14, 2016, https://hbr.org/2016/07/what-great-listeners-actually-do.

7. Ralph G. Nichols and Leonard A. Stevens, "Listening to People," *Harvard Business Review*, September 1957.

8. Rebecca Solnit, *Men Explain Things to Me* (Chicago: Haymarket Books, 2015).

9. Charlotte England, "Men Call Sweden's Mansplaining Hotline to Mansplain Why They Don't Like It," *The Independent,* November 22, 2016, www.independent.co.uk/news/world/europe/sweden-mansplaining-hotline-sexist-men-dominate-lines-blocked-for-women-colleagues-a7431201.html.

10. Zach Brittle, "Turn towards Instead of Away," *The Gottman Institute*, April 1, 2015, https://www.gottman.com/blog/turn-toward-instead-of-away/.

The Future: Raising Better Men

1. Raquel Fernández, Alessandra Fogli, and Claudia Olivetti, "Mothers and Sons: Preference Formation and Female Labor Force Dynamics," *Quarterly Journal of Economics* 119, no. 4 (November 2004): 1249–1299.

2. Claire Cain Miller and illustrations by Agnes Lee, "How to Raise a Feminist Son," *New York Times*, June 1, 2017, https://www.nytimes.com/2017/06/02/upshot/how-to-raise-a-feminist-son.html.

3. Dale Spender, *Man Made Language* (London: Pandora, 2001).

4. Brian Heilman, Gary Barker, and Alexander Harrison, *The Man Box: A Study on Being a Young Man in the US, UK, and Mexico* (Washington, DC, and London: Promundo-US and Unilever, 2017).

5. Alice Robb, "How Gender-Specific Toys Can Negatively Impact a Child's Development," *New York Times*, August 12, 2015.

Acknowledgments

I've pretty much spent my whole life making stuff no one really needs; ephemeral playthings for people with discretionary time and income to twitch, click, and tweet away. This book is my attempt to engage more meaningfully in the business sphere.

I want to thank the women leaders and entrepreneurs who shared with me their insights and continue to inspire us all. Lisa Maki, Pam David, Erika Trautman, Niniane Wang, Cheryl Yeoh, Melody McCloskey, Shelley Ross, Laura Parmer-Lohan, Adriane Brown, Maha Ibrahim, Debbie Landa, Bridget Frey, Penny George, Charlotte Guyman, Christina Watt, Dr. Ellie Guardino, and Kristen Hamilton contributed valuable time and personal stories to make the important issues in this book come alive. May you readers benefit from their sage wisdom, as I have immeasurably.

And, in some cases, women contributed stories but requested to be anonymous. In those cases, we have used first names only and removed personal details. But your stories are still powerful contributions, and I thank you also for your contributions.

I could not have written this book without Grace Kahng. She is the quarterback from whom I hear all audibles and the navigator who is unafraid of choppy waters. Her editorial instincts are nothing short of masterful, refining and reshaping cloddish ideas into those worthy of publication. She is the very model of the kind of effective blended leadership that I speak of, and I honestly don't know how she does what she does so dang well, all the time.

I thank my colleagues Karen Cooper and Molly Shapiro, who contributed thoughtful edits and encouraged me to humanize this book with personal stories. Ana Fleming fact-checked the hell out of the manuscript, following my side notes and recollections back to authoritative research and reportage.

My editor at John Wiley & Sons, Jeanene Ray, is the believer. Despite my amateur confusion around timelines, production sequencing, and book marketing, Jeanene has been the perfect editor, never doubting for a minute that "Team Better Together" would deliver. And working with Danielle Serpica, Caroline Vincent, and Peter Knox of Wiley has been a similar pleasure and honor.

Most important, heaps of gratitude go to my wife, Heather, who set the high bar for patience, teamwork, and tolerance while I wrote this book. Her living example of strong female power has opened my mind to behaviors and attitudes that were subtly sexist both at my companies and at home, and it is she who deserves the lion's share of credit for raising a feminist son and offering a glimpse of a most hopeful future to come.

The Better Together Pledge

As a business leader, CEO, board member, VC, manager, business owner or employee of either gender, I pledge to work intentionally to advance gender equality in my place of work, to actively develop and promote women into positions of leadership, to speak out against bias, and to not tolerate sexual harassment, so that we can all work Better Together.

Specifically, I pledge to:

1. Remove Bias Against Women in Recruiting

2. Fully Support Women's Development within my Organization

3. Listen Louder and Support Women's Communication

4. Create a Family-Forward Work Culture

5. Not Tolerate Sexual Harassment regardless of Perpetrator's Performance

6. Adopt the ERA's Language for my Organization

7. Encourage Women to Support Women

8. Set the Right Example for the Next Generation

For more details please go to www.jsposato.com/pledge

Index